# ICONOCLASM

TONY ZORC

# ICONOCLASM

## A SURVIVAL GUIDE IN THE POST PANDEMIC ECONOMY

ForbesBooks

Published by ForbesBooks, Charleston, South Carolina.
Member of Advantage Media Group.

ForbesBooks is a registered trademark, and the ForbesBooks colophon is a trademark of Forbes Media, LLC.

Printed in the United States of America.

10 9 8 7 6 5 4 3 2 1

ISBN: 978-1-95086-335-8
LCCN: 2020924061

Cover and Layout design by David Taylor.

This custom publication is intended to provide accurate information and the opinions of the author in regard to the subject matter covered. It is sold with the understanding that the publisher, Advantage|ForbesBooks, is not engaged in rendering legal, financial, or professional services of any kind. If legal advice or other expert assistance is required, the reader is advised to seek the services of a competent professional.

 Advantage Media Group is proud to be a part of the Tree Neutral® program. Tree Neutral offsets the number of trees consumed in the production and printing of this book by taking proactive steps such as planting trees in direct proportion to the number of trees used to print books. To learn more about Tree Neutral, please visit **www.treeneutral.com**.

Since 1917, Forbes has remained steadfast in its mission to serve as the defining voice of entrepreneurial capitalism. ForbesBooks, launched in 2016 through a partnership with Advantage Media Group, furthers that aim by helping business and thought leaders bring their stories, passion, and knowledge to the forefront in custom books. Opinions expressed by ForbesBooks authors are their own. To be considered for publication, please visit **www.forbesbooks.com**.

# CONTENTS

# INTRODUCTION

## What Just Happened?

In March of 2020, most of the world—along with our politicians—panicked. When presented with an unfamiliar threat in the form of a novel coronavirus, life as we knew it shut down. In the United States, businesses shuttered, schools closed—even medical procedures deemed "nonessential" grinded to a halt. While panic is never a desirable response, it is the predictable response when you have never prepared or been trained to get through a certain conflict.

In a way, to me the coronavirus pandemic has felt similar to a natural disaster. I grew up in the midwestern United States, in metropolitan Chicago, and I have lived most of my adult years on the East Coast, in Maryland. As a result, I have been through many tornadoes and hurricanes and, especially in my school years, received a lot of training on how to handle and survive such a disaster. Chicago schools regularly had scheduled tornado drills. The school would sound an alarm; we would walk—not run—into the school hallway and kneel down with our heads against the inner support wall of the building and lace our hands together, covering the back of our neck. Our teachers would actually critique our form and instruct us regarding our tornado sheltering technique to inform us if we were doing it correctly or not. Although I, along with my schoolmates, would often mock these exercises, I felt very thankful for this training years later when a real tornado hit us. But when everything shut down in March 2020, not one average American citizen had ever received any kind of preparation instruction for what to do in the event of a global pandemic.

Similarly with natural disasters like tornadoes and hurricanes, there is a categorization system from zero to five so you know how severe they are, evaluating damage indicators, environmental factors, and potential human risk. We also have ratings for air quality—pollen and allergens—yet nothing for viruses and widespread, easily transmutable human illnesses to help us understand the degree of risk we are taking when venturing out into the proverbial public interaction storm.

So when the whole world's attention turned toward the coronavirus, most of us had never even heard of the term *social distancing* before, had never contemplated wearing a mask outside of a surgical suite for any reason other than maybe a random home-improvement painting project—I certainly hadn't. We needed a pandemic protocol—something we trained for as a society and even performed drills for. Just as we keep flood and tornado kits, we should have had stock bundles of masks and hand sanitizer for use when the coronavirus pandemic reared its ugly head. There should have been a scale of severity to help manage our collective perspective of the potential risks.

The good news is we're starting to make those adjustments and formulate a pandemic protocol, but it's unfortunately been at the sky-high price of a prolonged economic shutdown. We've learned when to wear masks, socially distance, and wash our hands. We identified what I call "temporary designated personal space," which is the concept of walking into a restaurant, hair salon, or gym with a mask on until you arrive at your table, chair, or station, where you can then remove it until you leave the space for any reason.

I predict that, even better, we are now preparing to be on the watch for future pandemics on a similar dimension as weather events, just like we do with air quality, allergens, rain, wind, etc. We will also most likely have ratings for pandemics to help us calculate the appropriate risk-reward activity when leaving our home to be in public spaces—a "Pandemic 1" may recommend social distancing of three feet and wearing masks when distancing is not practical, and a "Pandemic 5" would probably mean you are not leaving the house for any reason and anyone who does is probably wearing something close to a space suit with its own oxygen tank. Since I have a diverse set of friends, colleagues, and employees, it was apparent to me that some of us thought of the COVID-19 pandemic as a "Pandemic 1" while others treated it like a "Pandemic 5." If we'd had a coordinated response from officials and a common definition of the severity of the situation, perhaps a lot of the economic and personal losses we experienced during the pandemic could have been mitigated, but unfortunately that just did not happen.

But it's easy to say in hindsight what we should have done, and the grave reality is no response like the one I just described took place. Without having a plan, we simply panicked and decided to stop everything. While we will not know the true impact of the US government's response to the coronavirus for years to come, we can begin to consider the factors and implications of that decision now.

To be clear, this book is not a political manifesto trying to lay blame as to who did what wrong, but instead it is an attempt to provide a framework of what to do now and to understand how we got here.

To those of you who lost loved ones to COVID-19, I extend my deepest condolences. I know what it feels like to lose someone suddenly, without warning. I lost my twenty-year-old son to heart failure on March 27 of 2019. Ethan was a fit runner attending York College of Pennsylvania when he passed away in the middle of the night. He died from SCD, or sudden cardiac death. Basically, the electrical system in his heart malfunctioned and went out. It was a complete shock the next morning when a local police officer came to the house with two social workers to inform us he had died.

When you have lost a loved one, there is not much anybody can say to comfort you. Please understand that my intent here in analyzing the pandemic and the way forward is not to minimize your loss. Rather, when it comes to the impact of the coronavirus—and the decisions it has driven federal, state, and local governments to make, I feel it's critical that we talk about the virus's death toll. My only goal is to put the numbers—current as of this writing—into perspective.

The reality is that the vast majority of people who have contracted this virus have not died. For the most part, those who have died of COVID-19 were elderly, already sick, or had compromised immune systems. Most of us have not perished or even faced significant risk of death. While this does not matter or bring comfort when you are the one who has lost somebody, it should affect policy and procedure on a larger scale.

It is plain to see that we are facing a grave new reality, one requiring significant economic recovery. Although I believe we will have learned from this panic and that future responses to challenges that arise will be tempered by the knowledge we have gleaned so far, our collective reaction to the virus points to one crucial factor: we as a society do not question what we are told—potentially to our own detriment.

Nonetheless, this book is not about pointing fingers and laying blame. It is about building an inquisitive spirit and forming our own opinions through critical thinking today and tomorrow. It is about considering how to achieve success in a new way going forward.

The strategies and insights here boil down to a single powerful concept: iconoclasm.

An iconoclast is someone who challenges the existing way of doing things, engineers a better approach, and then implements it. Being an iconoclast is really about improving your life and the lives of others. Iconoclasts are always looking to reach new heights in all areas of life, as they are constantly finding new opportunities wherever they focus their thoughts. Iconoclasm is about unlocking doors that seem to be shut—and ushering everyone through them. That kind of approach is the key to unlocking success in the current and post-corona panic economy.

But before we get there, we have to understand how we as a society got *here*—deep into a nationwide panic attack.

# The Anatomy of a Panic Attack

A nation is really just a group of people, and just as a single person can have a panic attack—which may cause them to make a series of irrational decisions and avoid people, places, work, and other triggering situations—so can a group of people. In March of 2020, the world collectively began panicking over the outbreak of the coronavirus. Let's analyze the anatomy of this particular panic attack, including the elements that have driven it to such great heights—especially in the United States.

## THE TWENTY-FOUR-HOUR NEWS CYCLE

Panic is a dream come true for today's media outlets. Every waking hour, we are drawn to the media, with chyrons streaming across the screen and side-panel charts informing us how many people have died each day from the virus. The message many outlets are blasting at us is that we are in grave danger of dying ourselves and killing others if we don't stay in isolation.

> Panic is a dream come true for today's media outlets.

Some channels, like CNN, seem to intensify the reporting of deaths of people under fifty, with the intent of striking more fear into the hearts of already anxious Americans. Don't write me off as a right-winger here: Fox News is just as bad! Across virtually every station, the facts are presented like a video game scoreboard.

Regardless of their political position, humans are wired to accept repetition as fact: whatever message we continue to tell ourselves is what we come to believe. Neuroscientific researchers have investigated whether affirmations—statements that focus on positivity and self-empowerment—actually change the brain. There is MRI evidence suggesting that certain neural pathways are strengthened when people practice self-affirmation tasks.[1] As Henry Ford famously said, "Whether you think you can, or think you can't—you're right."

Athletes and professionals who have achieved any level of success know this to be true. Many great athletes, like Michael Jordan, Kobe Bryant, and Muhammed Ali, have professed that success comes from blocking out everything negative while they bring to reality the positivity they first created in their mind. To achieve, we must focus on affirmations like "I can do it," "I am only limited by constraints I place on myself," and "I will survive and thrive if I focus and work hard."

But just as we have the ability to think our way into success and achievement with the repetition of affirmations, we have the same capability to drive ourselves into a state of fear and isolation with the wrong messaging—such as those fed to us by the media.

## CORPORATE EVENT CANCELLATIONS

The second contributor to our panic started on February 27, when Facebook canceled its F8 conference, an annual meeting that brings together developers and entrepreneurs from around the world. This single event set the corporate precedent for meeting cancellations globally, and the entertainment and sports industries quickly followed suit, postponing or canceling shows and games around the world. It's not that I disagree with their decisions; I canceled my own company's corporate trade show, scheduled for April of 2021. However, the rapid-fire shutdown of events drove our anxiety sky high, further fueling our collective panic in a very short period of time.

---

1   Christopher Cascio et al., "Self-Affirmation Activates Brain Systems Associated with Self-Related Processing and Reward and Is Reinforced by Future Orientation," *Social Cognitive and Affective Neuroscience* 11, no. 4 (April 2016): 621–29, doi: 10.1093/scan/nsv136.

## SOCIETAL SENSITIVITY

Our societal tendency to be overly sensitive is another contributor to widespread panic. Why? Since the 1990s, our collective sensitivity has challenged our ability to have healthy public debates. While respect for one another's heritage, suffering, and experiences are paramount to successful interactions, we lose the ability to have productive discourse when we can't speak without the intense fear of offending someone with a poor choice of words. When it comes to the coronavirus, many of those who spoke in interest of the economy early on in the pandemic had to contend with the potential of being labeled tone deaf, insensitive, or even heartless.

As a result of our culture's tight grip on political correctness, even after a few weeks of lockdown, the idea of returning to work with social distancing and safety precautions in place was grossly underrepresented in the national debate. This lack of representation in the conversation essentially led to an economic shutdown, which only fueled more panic among citizens, who now worried not only about their health but also about their financial well-being.

## A LACK OF PRESIDENTIAL LEADERSHIP

A lack of leadership in the highest echelons of government has been yet another contributor to our nationwide panic attack. Although President Trump was clearly pushing to reopen the economy from the pandemic's onset, he failed to lead us through the pandemic with a unified, coordinated national response. While his plan was mostly to ignore it and downplay it, unfortunately the American public was too scared to accept this approach. We needed someone to address the pandemic head-on. The lack of unity and a centralized plan fed the flames of panic, conveying to the public that our ship seemed to be missing a captain at the helm as we sailed into the storm.

While his daily press briefings at the beginning of the pandemic could have been an opportunity to cultivate calm and hope, instead President Trump used them to promote his achievements, redirect responsibility, and bring attention to his campaign for reelection.

## THE ABSENCE OF A RISK-REWARD ANALYSIS

In the absence of presidential leadership, we found ourselves searching for others to take on that role. In the first weeks and months of the pandemic, Bill Gates, among others, emerged as a national leader of sorts in this time of crisis, appearing as a guest on talk shows and newscasts and warning us of the threat of the virus.

I have the utmost respect for Mr. Gates, and, like most business professionals, I admire his wealth and see him as one of the world's smartest men. But he and others who shared similar messaging heightened our sense of panic and contributed to the dysfunction of our shutdown.

Of course, I do not speak for Mr. Gates, but I am speculating that his aim was for us to take the virus seriously, adopt physical distancing, and shelter in place for a period of time to flatten the curve—a logical approach. Judging by his philanthropic efforts, I believe Mr. Gates was focused on a global approach with regards to the eradication of the virus and ensuring the safety of everyone on the planet. But as time goes on, we find ourselves running into some issues with that particular strategy.

While I applaud this effort and initiative, we must realize that there is risk involved in navigating a public health crisis. A functioning economy can't be based on complete and total safety for everyone. Moreover, the economic crisis we have created is much larger and far reaching than the safety risk at hand. At this point, its legacy will eclipse that of the coronavirus. Where Bill Gates had the opportunity but failed us as a leader was in not helping us through a risk-reward analysis of the pandemic when we needed a leader to do this more than ever.

## UNPREPAREDNESS

No nation on earth was prepared for this pandemic. In the United States, despite having one of the most respected medical systems at our disposal, we had no actionable plan to manage a pandemic—nor the right equipment and protection for healthcare workers. Aides from both the Bush and Obama administrations have come forward claiming there were government operational plans for a pandemic, but the reality is either the plans were not relevant enough to the current situation or the current government was just too dysfunctional to find them and broadcast them. Either way, the result was unpreparedness. That unpreparedness, regardless of who is to blame, was a huge contributor to our national panic.

We should not have had to waste time figuring out how to manage this pandemic. A set of rules and protocols for this type of situation should have been outlined in detail by the government. Had we been prepared at all, the public could have spent a week learning the behaviors necessary to operate safely, and we could have avoided a full shutdown. After all, there is no historical basis for such a decision.

# The Impact of Our Panic-Induced Shutdown

There are many diseases that we don't fully understand, but never in the history of the world have we shut down entirely. With yellow fever, polio, the Spanish flu, H1N1, and Ebola, we used what we knew about their spread to avoid them while continuing to live our lives. Even with the outbreak of the Spanish flu, which infected five hundred million people and killed roughly fifty million individuals, we never shut down our economy—and simultaneously balanced our response to the disease with our efforts in World War I.

But in this day and age, we have traded a fear of contracting the virus and dying for certain economic disaster, a reality worth panicking about. The grave economic impact of this event is extremely real and visible in three major ways:

- **Doing tremendous damage to the country's GDP.** According to the Commerce Department, the United States' gross domestic product, which captures overall economic health, fell at an annual rate of 33 percent as of Q2 2020 due to our reaction to the virus. As of this writing, economists estimate that shutdowns across the country will most likely yield an annual decline consistent with this rate by the end of 2020.[2]

- **Raising the United States' already dangerously high debt levels.** National debt was at nearly $25 trillion prior to the pandemic. Congress approved an additional $2.4 trillion in coronavirus relief for industries, small businesses, and individuals. That kind of aid cannot be sustained—the government can't keep paying people not to work. The fall of empires comes when they declare bankruptcy. This happens when they can't continue to pay their debt and interest payments with the cash they have, requiring them to print extra money to do so. The currency devaluation causes a chain reaction

---

2   "U.S. Economy Shrank at 5% Annual Rate in the First Quarter," *CNBC Markets*, May 28, 2020, https://www.cnbc.com/2020/05/28/us-gdp-q1-2020-second-estimate.html.

that can destroy the economy—and the empire—in a matter of weeks.

- **Further deepening the economic divide.** There is no doubt that wealth inequality has been on the rise in our country for more than thirty years. Shutting down the economy has been most destructive to small businesses. The *Washington Post* estimated that over one hundred thousand businesses will be gone permanently due to the shutdown, despite Congress approving trillions of dollars to rescue them.[3] The chance to own a small business and watch it prosper is truly the modern American dream, and with each week of closure, so many have found that dream delayed or destroyed. Meanwhile, wealthier families and those with larger businesses who are able to weather the storm will only grow more powerful as they absorb their newly bankrupted competition.

Of course, it is not only our economy that has been affected by the shutdown. In addition to the economic impact of widespread closures, we must also consider the effects on our mental health. According to the Kaiser Family Foundation, nearly half of adults have reported a deterioration in their mental health due to stress and worry over the shutdown.[4] The isolation inherent in a closed economy and a lack of socialization has driven loneliness, anxiety, and depression to record highs. If anything, the shutdown has taught

---

3    Heather Long, "Small Business Used to Define America's Economy. The Pandemic Could Change That Forever," *Washington Post*, May 12, 2020, https://www.washingtonpost.com/business/2020/05/12/small-business-used-define-americas-economy-pandemic-could-end-that-forever/.

4    Ashley Kirzinger, Audrey Kearney, Hiz Hamel, and Mollyann Brodie, "KFF Health Tracking Poll—Early April 2020: The Impact of Coronavirus on Life in America," Kaiser Family Foundation, April 2, 2020, https://www.kff.org/coronavirus-covid-19/report/kff-health-tracking-poll-early-april-2020/.

us that we as a species are not meant to live on our own. We were made to live in community with one another.

In addition, some have found themselves trapped in dangerous situations. In homes where domestic violence has been an issue, victims have most likely suffered more abuse than ever before, with lockdowns leading to mounting tensions. In early April of 2020, less than a month after lockdowns began in much of the United States, nine of the country's largest police departments reported double-digit jumps in domestic violence calls and incidents.[5]

There is no doubt in my mind that we have very smart American companies and engineers who will solve this problem long term. The same goes for other countries in the world. Just like we restructured airport security after 9/11, we will now take precautions and build systems to handle pandemics in the future. However, we should have kept the economy going while we built the long-term solution this time around. In failing to do so, we've set ourselves up for a challenging recovery. With that in mind, let's take a look at what the recovery looks like.

## What Does the Recovery Look Like?

Beginning in late March 2020 and early April of 2020, the concept of a V- or U-shaped economy started to surface in the mainstream media. This is the idea that the economy is going to come roaring back at a unprecedented pace, unlike any other recession we've had in history. While this message provides a lot of hope during a time of great pain and fear, unfortunately such an outcome is unlikely. Let's

---

5    Sarah Al-Arshani, "Nine Large Metro Police Departments Report 'Double-Digit Percentage Jumps' in Domestic Violence 911 Calls as More People Shelter at Home," *Business Insider*, April 6, 2020, https://www.businessinsider.com/as-the-coronavirus-pandemic-grows-so-does-domestic-violence-2020-4.

keep in mind that the Great Depression of the 1930s lasted a solid ten years, despite no businesses being forced to close, and arguably only ended with the United States' entry into World War II. In September of 2020, the concept of a K-shaped economy started surfacing in media outlets, indicating that our economic divide between rich and poor is only going to widen with the recovery. While the rich will get richer, the poor and middle class will do worse than before.

Every other recovery from recession has had different drivers than this one. Whatever you believe and whether or not it's backed by data or science, it's really just anyone's guess at this point.

To give you some reference, the gross domestic product (GDP) of the United States, currently the world's largest economy, is a pretty good measure for the health of the economy in this instance. Looking at the natural history of the GDP and how it has changed over the years, without any influence from worldwide natural disasters and wars, the average contraction in GDP in the United States since World War II has occurred in 11.1 months. In other words, going from the peak of GDP to the bottom, or trough, in an economic cycle since 1945 has taken forty-seven weeks, or 11.1 months naturally. Unfortunately this contraction will probably take longer than the 11.1-month average, with most public school systems going 100 percent virtual in fall of 2020 and payroll protection plans running out. So it is likely that the bottom of this economic cycle will be sometime in mid- to late 2021, making this a sixteen-to-twenty-month contraction. The depth of the contraction is what is most disturbing. The GDP contraction in Q2 of 2020 was 32.9 percent. This was more than three times as deep as the previous record, set in 1958, and four times as deep as the worst quarter of the Great Recession.

Natural expansions—the time it takes for the GDP to travel from trough to peak—typically take about five years. However this data is based on an open economy. The prolonged shutdown means that there will be no recognizable recovery, as it will occur over the course of ten to twenty years—such a long period of time that we won't even think of it as such. Instead, we will become used to a new "depression-pandemic" norm and to living under those conditions for years.

But we have options in terms of how we move forward. We don't have to do things in the manner they have always been done. In fact, it would behoove us to do something quite different. This book is going to help you figure out your own new normal and path for recovery—not just for yourself but for those you may lead.

## What Are Existing Paradigms—and Why Don't we Challenge Them?

There seems to be a prescription for most things we do in life. This includes a wide range of activities and exercises, from simple to complex, from easy to hard, from matter-of-fact to deeply emotional:

- What we eat
- What we wear
- How we exercise
- How we shop for a product
- What schools we choose to attend
- How we choose our career
- How we get our first job
- How we move up the corporate ladder
- How we manage people
- How we launch and grow our businesses

- How we create a corporate mission statement

- Where we buy a home

- How we choose a political party

- How we care for ourselves medically

Why do so many of us tend to operate in the same way? Most of us let others think through what is best for us and readily accept their vision. We don't bother to challenge the paradigm they have established.

We don't think to question what we are told because from our earliest days on the planet, our parents told us what to do. They cared for us, instructed us, and warned us of approaching danger. They taught us how to act, what to believe, and who to trust. In essence, we learned to trust them first and foremost. Since we are raised with people who seem to know all the answers to our questions, it is easy to just continue to assume someone else has already thought things through.

We make these assumptions of the government as well. When it came to COVID-19, most of us assumed the government had thought through preventative measures and rules to help keep us safe in the case of a pandemic.

Unfortunately, some of us even grew up in homes where our parents didn't want us to think independently. They believed a controlling approach kept their kids safer, so they discouraged their children from thinking for themselves and even punished them when they did. With that kind of model, it's not uncommon to raise our own children the same way—making it a multigenerational problem.

It is unfortunate that several government administrations and departments have the same desire: to prevent independent thought in order to enforce their own agenda.

It is only when a parent intentionally persuades and coaches their child to think for themselves that they begin to do so—and that takes time and effort. Having four children of my own, I have fallen into the trap of busyness and forming a time-crunched routine. Many of us have been caught running on the parent treadmill with a cycle of pushing our kids through school, sports and extracurriculars, dinner, homework, and bed. The weekends can be just as bad in terms of shuttling the kids between social activities, tournaments, and concerts and hounding them to do chores. Life just gets busy as we get caught running on the treadmill from one thing to the next.

One of the greatest gifts my father provided me was coaching, training, encouragement, and rewards when I demonstrated that I was thinking for myself. I feel that my ability to be a successful iconoclast stems from him. Thank you, Stan! Though he passed away in 2007 from prostate cancer, I am attempting to ensure that his iconoclastic legacy lives on through me.

With that in mind, let's talk a little bit more about where we tend to run into roadblocks when it comes to independent thinking.

The reality is that from a very early age, most of us form a habit of doing as we are told blindly, without asking any questions. By not challenging the existing paradigm, we are losing out on huge opportunities to find what's best for us personally, for our communities, and for society at large. We are losing out on the opportunity to invent new ways of doing things and to pave a new and better path for ourselves and for others.

The good news is this habit is reversible; it can be replaced with a new paradigm. Becoming an iconoclast is a skill that you can build, just like any other skill—and it begins with thinking in a new way. With practice, you will start to do it unconsciously and automatically.

Here, I will reveal the iconoclast formula, a well-established and proven strategy that leads to success, efficiency, and wealth. Companies and nations alike have begun to apply this formula and recognize its undeniable power. But to truly understand its potential, let's consider context—the situations in which one might apply these concepts.

## The Value of Context

It is easy to proclaim such axioms as these:

- Success on Wall Street is achieved by buying low and selling high.

- The best way to start a business is to find an unmet need in the marketplace and fill it.

- When you establish the right leadership and goals within your organization, you will find success.

All these axioms are widely accepted to be true, but it is the specific details and circumstances with which they are applied that provide real insight. A specific example is a person who bought low and sold high on Wall Street. Someone who identified a unique unmet need in the marketplace and became a successful business-person. An individual who shared the exact criteria they used to find the right leader and meet their goals. That kind of information is the true treasure.

Why? It is through reading and learning from other people's specific stories that we figure out our own unique path to success. I have learned to be successful by hearing the stories of other success-ful people. In learning about their achievements, I'm often able to extract a principle that is applicable to my life. That's what makes all the difference.

With that in mind, I'd like to tell you a bit about who I am and how I got here.

# Who Is Tony Zorc?

I am a person who is comfortable with change. I would even say that my greatest strength is my ability to adapt. In fact, my success is rooted in my ability to adapt as soon as I see a process out of alignment with its underlying dynamics—which is almost always earlier than everyone else.

That tendency encouraged me to start a company, Accounting Seed, with no money and no outside investment. As of this writing, I've grown it into a well-established operation with one thousand customers, fifteen thousand users, and a multimillion-dollar valuation—all in ten years. I did it while maintaining a home, enriching a second marriage, parenting two biological children and two stepchildren, managing a difficult ex-spouse, staying physically fit, and growing my spiritual life.

How? By becoming an iconoclast and using the principles in this book. Here I share my journey using the iconoclast formula, including how I applied the formula to achieve success. Your journey will be different from mine, but the specific examples I provide from my life will give you the power to create your own success story.

Adopting the principles in this book will change your entire outlook on life and give you a new framework for success in the post-pandemic era. You'll have a new skill set that will allow you to see opportunities in any and all areas to which you apply it. This book covers the art of finding the opportunity, making a plan to take advantage of it, and taking action to bring that plan to fruition. Ultimately, it's about the combination of creativity, engineering, and action. All three go hand in hand to achieve success.

## WHY DID I WRITE THIS BOOK?

I think why an author writes a book is an extremely important question to ask. So many authors—especially in the business space—are just writing a book to promote themselves as an expert in a certain domain. The book is essentially a marketing instrument to advertise their services. It is very obvious, in most cases, when the author is doing this. It is why so many business books are poorly written—often by ghostwriters—and therefore not read.

I wrote this book. I did not use a ghostwriter. I did use an editor to review my work and coach me on my communication style and flow, but the book was entirely written by me. And let me tell you, it is a lot of work to write a book!

> I'm writing this book because I want to help change the way you think, plan, and act in our current and post-pandemic world and in your life.

Yet if I get any money from this book, I believe it will be a fractional return on the investment of my time compared to what I could get if I were to spend it focusing on my business. I already have a profit-producing enterprise, and as an iconoclast, I see a number of ways to expand it—with the limited resources being my time and energy. I don't need this book to help me get work or sell my product. Again, my purpose is bigger. Ultimately, I hope this book will help you find yours.

I'm writing this book because I want to help change the way you think, plan, and act in our current and post-pandemic world and in your life. I feel that it is my mission in life to do this for as many people as I can. I am hoping this book is a vehicle for you to start to rethink your decision process in all areas of life. I believe this will lead to more happiness for you, our society, and our environment. I believe it will have a ripple effect, influencing those you touch and encouraging them to do the same.

## THE ELEVATOR PITCH

If I needed to describe this book to you during an elevator ride, it comes down to this: this book is about how to find an opportunity, engineer a plan for change, and take action in a world that is constantly shifting. It calls out the fact that most activities we partake in are based on an established way of doing things and that many of us are not taught to think independently—and thus aren't very good at it. As such, we let others think for us. But it doesn't have to be that way.

Being an iconoclast is a learned skill, and the more you do it, the better you get. Many iconoclast journeys begin with frustration. In fact, that may be why you picked up this book. And it can help you find a better way.

# Harnessing Opportunity in a Changing World

The underlying dynamics of power are changing constantly in our lives and around the world. The coronavirus pandemic is a recent and significant change—but change is always constant and always relative to different people's life circumstances. A small change in technology or law may affect a physician's work and life enormously while having virtually no impact on the life of the accountant. These dynamics of power are creating new opportunities all the time and making old operating models and paradigms obsolete. As an iconoclast, I love this reality. You can learn to love it too, because it presents you with more opportunity than ever to be an agent of change for your own benefit and that of others.

Together, we will identify the shift in underlying societal dynamics created by the coronavirus and discuss the opportunities that have arisen or disappeared as a result. We'll dig into what the future could look like if we were to take an iconoclastic approach—as individuals and as a society. When you learn to think like an iconoclast, far more opportunities become available to you. Each will provide you with the chance to level up.

I first heard the term *level up* from my son Ethan while he was playing his Microsoft Xbox in 2017 with his friends. The concept of moving to the next level in the game, or leveling up, is especially fitting to how I view achievement in life. This is due to the fact that in the game, when you unlock the next level you don't lose access to the levels you already completed. You can return to these levels at any time. You essentially accumulate wealth by acquiring access to more levels without having to sacrifice anything. Put simply, iconoclasm has a ripple effect for the better.

I've mentioned the iconoclast formula, which I'll share in the next chapter. This formula will show you

- how to analyze the prescribed way,

- understand why it is the way it is,

- determine if the underlying dynamics of power have changed, and

- decide if a new opportunity is worth taking for you.

Ready to change your perspective, your life, and that of others around you? Read on.

# Part 1 Summary and Questions

## CHAPTER SUMMARY

- Our country reacted with panic to the coronavirus for a variety of reasons, creating an economic disaster that we will feel for the long term—most likely over a decade or longer.

- As such, challenging the existing way of doing things to form a sustainable new normal for yourself and those you lead is more necessary now than ever before.

## QUESTIONS TO CONSIDER

- What existing paradigms do you subscribe to without question?

- When was the last time you questioned guidance given to you by the media, government, or a company?

# PART 2

# WHAT IS AN ICONOCLAST?

An iconoclast is an individual who challenges the prescribed or established way of doing things, finds a better way, creates a plan for change, and executes it. Their thoughts and actions are a product of three fused factors: creative thinking, engineering and discipline, and the drive to make things better.

An iconoclast is a rugged individual. A bold thinker who doesn't give a hoot what tradition calls for. A person challenging the prescription or established norm. They are someone who sees options that other people can't or won't see. They break old paradigms and create new ones. Sometimes they can come off as rebels; however, a true iconoclast is still trying to achieve the same desired outcome as the old way of operating: success. They are not trying to derail the traditional way maliciously or for entertainment. Rather, they are typically attempting to solve the problem in an unorthodox way that somehow supersedes the manner in which things have always been done.

An iconoclast can be of any age, race, gender, or religious background. They can work in any industry and hold any job function. They are simply seeking something better. Most iconoclasts are curious people. The most successful iconoclasts are ones who follow up on their curiosity and do some research to vet their means to an end—reading, watching, and talking to people about why things are the way they are and their ideas for change. How does one become an iconoclast? In some ways, it's pretty simple.

## The Iconoclast Formula

I've developed a three-step process—what I call the iconoclast formula—to begin thinking and acting independently. Each step is summarized in the table below. I will go into further detail following the table below:

| STEP | STEP SUMMARY | STEP DESCRIPTION |
|------|--------------|------------------|
| 1 | Ask why. | Identify the prescribed or established way. Recognize the historical underlying dynamics supporting it, if they have changed, and if there are opportunities to do something different—and better. |
| 2 | Make a plan. | Create a plan for change with a vision of the outcome and set a "go live" date. |
| 3 | Execute it. | Execute the plan. |

Let's break things down a little further, beginning with the first step.

# Ask Why

You can identify the prescribed or established way regarding the subject matter you're analyzing by asking the following questions:

- How has this process been done in the past?

- What framework or rules are in place that drive the current way of doing things?

- How have most people addressed this issue or problem?

- How are most people recommending I solve this?

- How do others say I should think about this subject matter?

- Do vendors in the subject matter area present their solution in context of a common problem?

- How are solutions to this problem typically advertised?

Determining the established way is often the easiest step in the iconoclast formula. Unless the subject area is in a state of flux, it is simply the way it has always been done or the way it is being presented to you now. Below is a list of subject matter examples and their prescribed ways prior to the application of technology. These are classic examples of how technology challenged the status quo to form a new way. Nowadays, the new way listed has become the prescribed way for many people.

| SUBJECT MATTER | OLD WAY | NEW WAY |
|---|---|---|
| Catching a cab | Call a cab company or yell and raise your hand as you stand on the street corner waiting for one to drive by. | Use Uber or Lyft on your mobile phone. |
| Vacation home | Buy a time-share or rent from the vacation homes listed in a particular area. | Easily rent exactly what you need when you need it, choosing from a wide selection—and coordinating directly with the owner—via Airbnb. |
| College | Go to college after high school and figure out what you want to do after graduation. | Skip college, get a job in technology, and further your education online as you work. |
| Finding a babysitter | Ask friends and neighbors if they know anyone. | Find providers on Care.com. |

## ICONOCLASTS PAY ATTENTION TO HISTORY

A key part of being an iconoclast—and asking why effectively—is being a student of history. Why? To answer the question of why things are the way they are now, you must understand the history of the beliefs, tools and resources available, politics, and environment related to the subject matter. For example, thorough answers to each of the following questions would include a significant historical component:

- Why is Tesla valued higher than any of the legacy American car companies?

- Why does the Federal Reserve System work as it does?

- Why did the United States move away from the gold standard for currency valuation?

- Why are there so many kids' sports with travel leagues?

- Why has the housing market gone up so much in San Francisco?

- Why are so many preteens on the social media site TikTok?

All the references above have a history of beliefs, laws, resources, labor, and environmental factors that led to the situation being the way it is today. It is a requirement that you understand the history behind the paradigm you are challenging, since you are looking for changes in the underlying dynamics of that paradigm. If you don't know

> **A key part of being an iconoclast—and asking why effectively—is being a student of history.**

the history, you won't be able to determine if an underlying dynamic has changed.

Don't be overwhelmed; the internet makes uncovering the history of even the most obscure subjects easier than ever before. The tools we have today make searches simple, lightning fast, and rich in content returned. You'll also notice that your historical knowledge starts to build on itself. For example, when you know about the history of local real estate prices, you'll also begin to see connections to many other subjects like the market for realtors; real estate taxes; and the history of businesses and industries located in your home city, state, or province.

## WHAT ARE DYNAMICS?

I've mentioned the role of underlying dynamics a few times. A dynamic is a power or force that is helping to shape the world. As the world is in a constant state of flux, underlying dynamics are constantly changing with it. New dynamics appear all the time, just as old ones are always fading away. Beliefs, tools, resources, political law, and the environment are all categories of dynamics, but there are many more. The table below provides a description of each of these categories. Let's go deeper with some descriptions and examples:

| DYNAMIC | DESCRIPTION |
|---|---|
| Beliefs | Common ideas we assume to be true as a society |
| Tools | Devices or systems used to improve a process |
| Resources | The availability of skilled labor and materials to create products and services and sustain life |
| Politics | Man-made laws to establish rights, ownership, and process |
| Environment | The condition of our planet, home, or domicile |

## Beliefs

Our beliefs drive the paradigms behind how we act and perform tasks. This in turn is part of what shapes the prescribed way of doing things. Some remain beneficial, while others do not. For example, it was not until the 1890s that the germ theory of disease was accepted universally by the scientific community. This is the notion that bacteria, viruses, and other microorganisms too small to be seen will create disease if introduced into the body.

Today, this is common knowledge. We don't second-guess it, and for the most part, the underlying dynamics have not shifted such that believing otherwise has value. Let's discuss some prescribed ways of doing things that have come as a result of germ theory:

- People wash their hands before leaving the bathroom.

- Medical practitioners scrub their hands incessantly and use sterilized equipment when performing surgery.

- We practice social distancing when an illness is going around, as with the coronavirus outbreak.

Now, let's look at some examples of historical prescriptions that our society once believed were true but are now known to be false.

## Common Beliefs We Thought Were True in the Last Five Hundred Years

- The earth is the center of the universe (until 1543).

- California is an island (until 1698).

- The size and shape of your head determines your behavior (until 1840).

- Washing your hands won't prevent disease (until 1850).

- Bad smells can make you sick (until 1854).

- Continents do not move (until 1912).

- The universe is static (until 1927).

- Different parts of your tongue pick up different tastes (until 1974).

- Asbestos is a great building material (until 1960).

- Babies under twelve months old don't feel pain (until 1987).

## Common Beliefs We Thought Were True in the Last Twenty Years That We Now Know to Be False

- A low-fat diet with lots of carbs is the key to losing weight.

- Cities will continue to decay as people flee for the suburbs.

- Russia will become a healthy democracy.

- The AIDS epidemic will get worse.

- The Nintendo Wii is the future of gaming.

## Tools

Let's next look at tools. Tools are devices or systems used to improve processes. The introduction or application of a new tool to an established way of doing things is one of the clearest examples of how we can challenge the prescribed way. Thousands of businesses and products have been invented and prospered based on this concept alone. New tools are being invented all of the time through improved science, engineering, and ingenuity. Here are some examples of tools that have had a tremendous impact on human lives over the course of history:

| CHISEL | TELESCOPE | POCKET WATCH | TELEVISION |
|---|---|---|---|
| Fishhook | Cooking pot | Eyeglasses | Smartphone |
| Level | Lathe | Rifle | Electric car |
| Pencil | Oil refinement | Microprocessor | Solar cells |
| Software | Programming languages | Artificial intelligence | Robots |

## Resources

Resources refer to the general availability of labor and materials we need to create products and services as well as sustain life. Resources are changing constantly, just like all other dynamics. This list includes examples of dynamics that are categorized as resources:

- The availability of clean drinking water

- Skilled laborers, such as computer programmers or machinists

- The physical strength of the average man

- The availability of precious metals like copper, gold, silver, and titanium

- The availability of nuclear materials like uranium and plutonium

- The supply of oil and fossil fuels

- The supply of natural gas

## Politics

Next let's look at politics. Political laws create or remove barriers for individuals or groups of individuals in owning resources and performing actions. Politics are constantly changing with the world as well. For example, labor unions for factory workers in the United States—which probably peaked in terms of strength in the 1950s— are not much of a force today, as there are so few factory workers in the United States. Here are some examples of changes in political laws:

| COUNTRY/YEAR | LAW | CHANGE |
|---|---|---|
| England/1835 | Cruelty to Animals Act | Outlawed cruelty to animals |
| USA/1865 | Thirteenth Amendment to the US Constitution | Abolished slavery |
| USA/1973 | *Roe v. Wade* | Legalized abortion |
| Canada/1984 | Canada Healthcare Act | Established nationalized healthcare in Canada |
| USA/2010 | *Citizens United v. Federal Election Commission* | Legalized super PACs in US presidential elections |
| EU/2018 | General Data Protection Rights (GDPR) | Changed legal rights over corporate use of personal data |

## Environment

The condition of our habitat and environment is also a constantly changing dynamic that creates new opportunities. As we have become painfully aware via COVID-19, our environment is fragile. It can change very quickly. With all changes, new opportunities are born. All the environmental conditions listed here are forces that already—or have the potential to—affect the way we do things as a society:

- Pollution
- Global warming
- Widespread sickness and disease
- Solar flares
- Hurricanes
- Earthquakes

- Meteors

- Nuclear war

- Cyberattacks

## Other Dynamics

Dynamics do not always fall into the categories above. The following list of items are other dynamics that could dictate or disrupt the prescribed way:

- A baby boom

- The average human life span

- A growing or shrinking global population

- Fascist governments and societies

- A lack of infrastructure to enforce laws

# Iconoclasts Are Ahead of the Curve

Although dynamics are changing quite often, our established ways of doing things are not in step with them. The truth is, most people don't like change. It is hard work cognitively and emotionally, and there is always the risk that the new way won't be any better. While most people feel like they are on a fixed game board, the iconoclast knows how to adapt the rules of the game. And people *will* change when someone takes the time to show them a better way. This is the true iconoclastic opportunity. But you must know *why* your way is better to make your case.

This is why it's so important to understand why the established way exists. This is where just letting your natural curiosity take over can lead you to read the right articles, talk to the right people, or simply make accurate observations.

For instance, the reason John D. Rockefeller was able to corner the oil market by 1880 is that there were no laws against selling your product at artificially low market prices to drive a competitor out of business and force them to sell you their operation. The lack of legal structure and demand for oil as a tool to power engines were the driving dynamics behind this situation.

Another example is when Microsoft was able to create a monopoly on operating systems for personal computers in the 1980s and 1990s. Since IBM did not have an interest in writing an operating system for its computers, the company let Bill Gates write and maintain ownership of an independent operating system on which their machines ran. The fact that Windows was a tool that all other software products required gave the company its power.

But being an iconoclast is not just about convincing other people of the need for a paradigm shift—it's also about making important progress in your own life.

# The Power of Leveling Up

As I mentioned earlier in the book, leveling up is the act of improving your lot in life without losing what you already have. Leveling up is done incrementally. Just like in a video game, when you complete a level and move on to the next one, you don't lose access to the levels that you've already passed. That new level simply becomes an added benefit over and beyond what you've already got. Think of leveling up as contributing to, rather than sacrificing, what you currently have. If in the process, you feel like you are losing something, you aren't leveling up—you are really just trading one thing for another.

Have you ever seen those guys at the circus spinning plates? They start spinning plates on a stick in their hand and then pass the plates to their knee and then their toe. They keep adding plates to the mix, spinning them all over their body, on their wrist, forearm, shoulders, and so forth. When you level up, you're able to successfully spin another plate without dropping the others.

Now, it might be OK to decrease an existing activity a bit to make room for new goals and new improvements. However, leveling up typically does not mean you drop the thing altogether. For example, if I want to free myself up to do some walking at night with my dog, I might decide to cut my cardio schedule a little bit, but I'm not going to drop my workouts all together.

If you've ever read Jim Collins's book *Good to Great*, you know about big hairy audacious goals, or BHAGs. BHAGs can be tricky, as it's very easy to set goals that you cannot achieve and then get upset when you in fact don't achieve them. Leveling up is a strategy to avoid this phenomenon. In fact, it's really the opposite of a BHAG. Instead of aiming for one monumental, transformative shift, you're accomplishing small incremental goals. It's more of a theory of constant improvement.

## HOW TO LEVEL UP

What I have found in particular is that going for small iterative and measurable improvements in a short period of time is much better than laying out goals and objectives over many months. If you're not in the software world, you may not have heard much about the agile development method. The agile method has become the standard for product development, outlining goals in two- to three-week sprints. Goal setters make sure their outcome is achievable in this time frame and set a number of objectives to measure against and meet. Short-term goals keep you focused on the here and now and drive action. Meanwhile, long-term goals are too easy to recalibrate and reschedule, thus limiting progress.

> **If your plan doesn't seem doable in the allotted period of time, you need to break your goal down into smaller bites or assess your ability to acquire more resources in the form of time, money, people, and materials.**

When making a plan to level up successfully, you need to think in terms of days and weeks. Break down the work into steps that can be achieved with the resources you have in a day. And then ask what can be achieved in a week with the resources you have in that period of time. If your plan doesn't seem doable in the allotted period of time, you need to break your goal down into smaller bites or assess your ability to acquire more resources in the form of time, money, people, and materials.

Here are some examples:

- If you're trying to write a book, it would be better to set a goal of writing five hundred words per day rather than aiming to be done with chapter 1 by the end of the month.

- If you're trying to lose ten pounds of weight to look good for the beach season in three months, you'd be better off setting a goal each day to limit your calories to 1,500 than to lose three pounds per month.

- If you are trying to make your spouse feel more loved in your marriage, it would be better to set a goal to do a small gesture of love and affection each week than plan an amazing Valentine's Day or couple's vacation in three months.

## WHAT IS LEVELING OFF?

Sometimes leveling up actually involves eradicating something from your regularly scheduled programming. It is the absence of the activity that improves your lot in life. In this case, we call it leveling off. Leveling off is often an appropriate strategy in the addiction space, when your goal is to stop smoking, taking drugs, or drinking.

Just like leveling up, leveling off must be done incrementally, in small doses. When I wanted to drop morning caffeine, I weaned myself off slowly rather than go cold turkey. I knew from experience that attempting to do it in one fell swoop just wouldn't work. In the past, I'd do it successfully for about two weeks, only to end up right back to where I was before.

To level off strategically, I set a goal to stop my caffeine consumption fifteen minutes earlier each day. Monday I would not have any caffeine after 8:45 a.m., and then Tuesday I would avoid it after 8:30 and on Wednesday at 8:15 and so on.

## BE A "LUPPER"

Leveling up is all about your personal ambition. You can make it habitual so it is something you end up doing without putting any thought into it. A few years ago, I hired an executive coach, who asked me a pretty pointed question. He asked, "What can you *not* stop doing no matter what?"

I explained that what I couldn't stop doing was wanting to make small, iterative improvements in all areas of my life. That's what gives me joy. I like to improve myself and my conditions whenever and wherever I can. It can be my business, fitness, diet, marriage, fatherly relationships, knowledge of fill-in-the-blank subject. I love improving it all bit by bit.

Leveling up means pushing yourself further today than yesterday.

And to keep doing it day after day after day. It's all about unlocking a new challenge, a new area of achievement. It's not necessarily about learning brand-new skills as much as it's about improving upon the ones you already have.

After I answered his question, my coach started calling me a "lupper," combining the two words "leveling" and "up" into one: lupper: "You're lupping," he would say. What he meant is that I'm addicted to getting to that next level, just like in that video game, where leveling up brings an incremental improvement in your status and your powers. And lupping is essential to being a successful iconoclast.

## Make a Plan

With all the factors that go into asking why and leveling up in mind, it's time to make a plan. A plan to level up first starts with identifying outcomes. It begins with asking these questions: "What is it I am looking to achieve?" "What is the vision?"

It then declares a day where the work to get there will take place. Let's call this day the "go live" date. Working backward from the go-live date, you list the major milestones needed based on the level of effort and timeline. The plan then lists the resources you need to achieve the outcome. In most cases, this is a traditional project plan.

There are several books that outline successful project planning, and now people obtain undergraduate college degrees and professional certification in this subject. But while there is a lot of educational material and certifications on project planning out there, a project plan does not need to be complicated. A spreadsheet tracking milestones and dates based on a reasonable level of effort is good enough in most cases. Engineering a plan without dates is just a dream, not a plan. Committing your goals to real dates when you'll take steps to accomplish them is what makes them achievable.

## Execute a Plan

A person who thinks to challenge the existing paradigm but does not create a plan for change—much less take any action—is an iconoclastic thinker or a dreamer.

A person who thinks to challenge the existing paradigm and creates a plan for change but does not take any action is an iconoclast wannabe.

Nike's famous slogan of Just Do It started in 1988 and is still referenced today. Taking the action and just doing what you dreamed about or planned to do is what it really means to be an athlete. By the same token, action is the defining characteristic of an iconoclast. Only when thinking and asking questions, planning, and execution are combined can someone actually achieve iconoclast status.

I have been an entrepreneur for twelve years as of this writing. I can't tell you the number of cocktail parties and barbecues I've been to where I get into a conversation with someone who wants to be an entrepreneur but has no plan and doesn't want to take any risks. I assure you the count is in the high hundreds. They will ask me about my experience and then start explaining their idea to me.

Afterward, I see the searching in their eyes. They are looking for me to be impressed with the fact that they thought of something clever. Their ideas may very well be innovative, but in reality, most of them are just dreaming. They may not like their current job or work situation, and they want a better life. Since they are intelligent and creative, they can think of alternative ways to serve customers and enter new markets.

However, when it comes time to lay a plan, there are no dates on the calendar. In terms of action, fear overrides any momentum, and they go back to doing their old way. They're simply too afraid of what would happen if they actually took a chance and failed. But a willingness to confront failure is an inherent part of the iconoclast formula too.

## Iconoclasts Take Risks—and Often Fail

Being an iconoclast does involve some risk. It's not always financial—sometimes it's not being socially accepted, which could lead to things like embarrassment, loss of relationships, or social isolation.

Unfortunately, these risks are part of the price you pay to be an iconoclast. Being an iconoclast is not right for everybody, and that is OK. There is value in iconoclastic thinking too. If you have promising ideas you know you won't act on, don't hesitate to share them. You just may run into an iconoclast who is willing to take the risk to bring them to life.

Remember, too, that even if you do everything right, it doesn't mean you'll be successful every time. The defining characteristics of iconoclasts are the creative thinking, planning, and execution, not necessarily the outcome. Iconoclasts will fail often as they attempt to level up.

Hopefully, after some trial and error, you will find yourself leveling up more frequently than you fail—but not always. However, in a way, every mistake or failure comes with important insight on what not to do. By process of elimination, you eventually find success. Thomas Edison tried and failed ten thousand times before he invented the light bulb. Some current and future iconoclasts will experience a similar fate.

Along the way, people may assume you're crazy. You yourself may even wonder if you've lost your mind from time to time. Ultimately, though, you can't care what people think or say. It can be hard, but in the end you'll have the last laugh when you find a better way. Don't listen to the naysayers! Keep focused on what you know to be true. When the world catches up, you'll find yourself at the top.

# Part 2 Summary and Questions

## CHAPTER SUMMARY

- An iconoclast fuses these traits: creative thinking, engineering and discipline, and a drive to make things better.

- Dynamics are forces in the world that are constantly changing, such as societal beliefs, tools, resources, politics, and the environment. With change comes opportunity—and iconoclasts recognize that.

- Leveling up occurs by making goals and plans to be carried out in short intervals—such as a day, week, or two weeks—via small, measurable improvements.

- Sometimes leveling up comes in the form of leveling off—or eradicating a behavior that doesn't serve you—such as in the case of addition.

- One is not an iconoclast unless they carry out each step of the iconoclast formula: ask why, make a plan, and execute it.

- Iconoclasts take risks and fail often but have the courage to carry on.

## QUESTIONS TO CONSIDER

- Do you often find yourself curious about how things work?

- Are you interested in history?

- Do you find yourself making plans for improvement in your career, fitness, or relationships?

- What in your life are you looking to improve upon right now?

- What daily, weekly and biweekly plans can you set to achieve small, measurable goals in these areas?

# ICONOCLAST CLARIFICATION

Let's dig a little deeper into what truly constitutes an iconoclast, beginning with what an iconoclast isn't.

## What Is a Drone?

The opposite of an iconoclast is what I call a "drone." A drone is someone who, by and large, does not think for themselves. They trust others to think for them. Rather than questioning why something is the way it is, they assume someone has already figured out the best way to do it—and thus, the process doesn't require any further consideration on their part.

## THE TWO TYPES OF DRONES

There tend to be two types of drones, each with their own rationale for behaving the way they do. Let's label them so we can better define them. We'll call the first group "out of habit" and the second group "out of survival."

> **The fact is, we are all drones out of habit or survival in various areas and times of our lives.**

Out-of-habit drones typically have the capacity and the intellectual capability to pose the question why but just get caught up in the treadmill of life and its corresponding routines. Due to their existing habits and responsibilities, they fail to form another vital one: to stop, think, and ask why.

Out-of-survival drones are simply too overwhelmed to challenge themselves to ask why. They often don't have the bandwidth to think through the history of the subject matter at hand or to do any research. While they may be brilliant, they just don't have the time to devote themselves to being an iconoclast in a particular subject.

The fact is, we are all drones out of habit or survival in various areas and times of our lives. To see how they play out, we can look at a few examples from my own life.

## A DRONE IN MY RELATIONSHIP

I've been an out-of-habit drone in my relationships. One of the most memorable times when I've let my habits get the best of me occurred in my early twenties, and it led to a huge mistake: getting married at a very young age. It was an out-of-habit decision that has had lifelong consequences.

In fact, I am still navigating the ramifications of this decision—a full twenty-five years later—as I am trying to coparent two teenage girls with the woman I married and subsequently divorced.

I met my first wife while attending Hope College in Holland, Michigan. When we got engaged in May of 1996, I was getting ready to graduate. She was still a sophomore. We had been dating for about eighteen months. At that point, it was the longest relationship I had ever had. I just figured that marriage was the logical next step since—based on my limited life experience—we had been together for so long. Our being together had become a habit, and I didn't question it.

With my graduation date looming, I figured I might as well start building a life similar to the one my parents had: getting married, buying a house, and having kids—in short order.

My thought process didn't go much beyond that. Wow, did not thinking have a cost! I should note that I love my second wife and kids so much that I would not change a thing if altering my history meant I would have never met them. However, the point remains: being a drone can have significant consequences.

With that said, it's not possible to be an iconoclast in every area of life, and that's OK. To see what I mean, let's look at another example.

## A DRONE IN TRAVEL DECISIONS

I have become an out-of-habit drone when it comes to air travel. In 2003, I moved to Maryland. I currently live about twenty minutes from the BWI Airport, which happens to be a Southwest Airlines hub. When I moved, I formed a habit of flying Southwest because every time I looked for plane tickets, the airline had the cheapest domestic flights. Eventually, I stopped looking for flights through other airlines. I automatically headed to Southwest's website, knowing there would be a wide variety of flights at low prices.

Last year, a friend of mine told me that I should reevaluate my strategy: Southwest was no longer the cheapest option; the other competitive airlines were offering flights that actually cost less. After a quick internet search, I saw that he was right. But I still fly Southwest. Why? I formed that habit long ago.

Further, as I've gotten busier professionally, booking with Southwest has become something I do out of survival. I just don't have the time to shop around for airfares. I've determined instead that my time is more valuable than the amount I'd save if I were to search for and find a cheaper flight. Whether I'm an out-of-habit or out-of-survival drone at this particular moment in time, the bottom line is I'm not choosing to be an iconoclast when it comes to booking air travel. I'm OK with being a drone in this particular area.

We were not made to challenge every paradigm and decision in every area and stage in our lives—doing so would be very difficult too. Time serves the limiting factor: there is just not enough of it to question absolutely everything. Since the world is such a big place and I believe we all were created for a special purpose, it is natural to be an iconoclast in your chosen area of expertise. If you are naturally curious about your primary field of study or work and want to know why aspects are the way they are, chances are you're focused on the right stuff. I have chosen to pursue an iconoclastic ideal in information technology and business management. In these areas, I am constantly challenging the way I—and others—do things. When it comes to fitness, nutrition, and building Legos, I maintain my iconoclastic approach—though to a lesser extent. Quite simply, they are important to me but not as important as IT and business management. In pretty much every other area, I choose not to be an iconoclast. "Thank God," say my wife and kids! That's OK too.

# Iconoclasts versus Other Types of Leaders

With that said, not everyone who is passionate about something—or who has a leadership role in it—is necessarily an iconoclast in that area, and vice versa. While many entrepreneurs, inventors, and philanthropists happen to be iconoclasts, not all iconoclasts are entrepreneurs, inventors, or philanthropists. Are you confused? Yes? Let's expand.

We have established that an iconoclast is someone who questions the typical way of doing things and asks why they are the way they are. They find a better way, lay a plan for change, and execute it. An iconoclast is someone who does these three things whether or not they are working in the context of business or technology. For example, an iconoclast could be

- a mother trying to better educate her child,

- a school principal attempting to effectively track student attendance,

- a software engineer looking to better deploy patches of code,

- a fitness trainer searching for a better way to track athlete performance,

- a doctor aiming to better diagnose a health condition, or

- an accountant trying to better reconcile a company bank account.

Let's take a closer look at some of the leadership roles that may or may not overlap with an iconoclastic approach.

## ENTREPRENEURS

An entrepreneur is someone who is willing to assume risk in a new business venture in terms of starting and financing it, with the expectation that they will receive something in return for their investment. While they must have a game plan for the business and a vision for its success, they don't necessarily have to generate the concept and plan themselves—nor do they even need to execute it. An entrepreneur can take someone else's ideas and hire a management team to carry it out. It is only the responsibility and risk that are essential components of their role.

## INVENTORS

An inventor is someone who creates a new product or service that did not previously exist. An inventor does not necessarily need to be an iconoclast. For example, when Thomas Edison invented the phonograph, there was no existing paradigm to challenge. It was just something that had never been done before.

In fact, most inventors are not iconoclasts. They are scientists and engineers trying to do something for the first time. What they aren't doing is challenging an existing system, protocol, or practice, a defining characteristic of an iconoclast.

## PHILANTHROPISTS

A philanthropist is someone who donates money, time, or resources for the benefit of a person or group of people in need. A philanthropist could be an iconoclast as well, but again, iconoclasm is not a requirement. The vast majority of philanthropists give their time and money in an already-established manner. Of course, there's nothing wrong with giving in a prescribed way—as long as it is based on altruism. With that said, just doing good for others does not make one an iconoclast.

Let's summarize:

| WHO | DEFINITION |
| --- | --- |
| Iconoclast | Someone who challenges the existing way of doing things, finds a better way, lays a plan to enact it, and executes the plan |
| Entrepreneur | Someone willing to assume a materially significant financial risk in a business venture in anticipation of a return on that investment |
| Inventor | Someone who creates something new, whether it be a process, strategy, product, or service |
| Philanthropist | Someone who donates money, time, or materials for the benefit of a person or group of people in need |

To clarify things further, I'd like to tell you the story of an icono-clastic product, how it was perceived and received by the public, and how that reception changed over time.

# An Iconoclastic Journey

In 1999, I took a job working for a company named Herman Miller. Herman Miller is in the office furniture manufacturing market. The company makes cubicles, office desks and chairs, file cabinets, and more—basically everything you would need to furnish a commercial office. Based in Holland, Michigan—just a stone's throw away from my alma mater—it is a fantastic organization in virtually every way imaginable. The company is well managed, innovative, profitable, and a great place to work. It has had happy customers for over one hundred years now.

Over the course of the past century, Herman Miller has dem-onstrated a lot of out-of-the-box thinking. The company has a rich history of being known as the "innovation company" in its industry. Herman Miller challenged the existing paradigm in the office furniture industry that dictated that the designer of a particular product should be employed by the company manufacturing the product.

Herman Miller does not employ any of its designers, and that has become one of the secrets to its success. This approach has allowed them to execute the most innovative ideas in the industry *and* give credit to those who came up with them—thus transforming their designers into celebrities. Charles and Ray Eames, whom the company worked with from the 1940s to the 1980s, are among their most famous contributors. And as a result of their unique approach and sterling reputation, the company has continued to attract the best and brightest of designers to this day.

Bill Stumpf was another famous designer for Herman Miller, crafting the legendary Aeron chair. Stumpf conducted research at the University of Wisconsin–Madison, working with specialists in orthopedic and vascular medicine to delve into ergonomics and build a chair that would optimize the way people sit.

Previously, office chairs were designed primarily based on aesthetics. The way they looked was so much more important to people than how comfortable they were to sit in. In many traditional office spaces, it was thought that the more grand the chair looked, the more important the person in it.

On the other hand, Bill Stumpf built the Aeron chair solely for comfort and ergonomics. He thought little about the look of it. What happened to the Aeron chair is a similar story to what happens to a lot of iconoclastic thinkers, products, and movements. They are often mocked, laughed at, and rejected when they first debut. But eventually, enough people come to appreciate their unique features and accept and respect their out-of-the-box nature as a result. At that point, they not only become appreciated but mainstream as well.

When the Aeron chair first launched in 1992, the product's sales were not that great. Herman Miller proceeded to do some marketing surveys to determine why and found out that buyers simply thought the chair looked ugly. They reported that its nontraditional appearance was throwing them off; to them, it didn't look very regal, not like something an executive would enjoy. Some people even said it looked like some kind of insect.

Herman Miller acknowledged that the chair was not the most aesthetically pleasing seating product on the market and tried to convince customers in traditional industries to overlook that fact and just try sitting in it. The company was convinced that once a customer tried it out, they would fall in love with function over form, accepting the aesthetics for what they were.

Herman Miller then decided that the chair would have to be sold and marketed to very forward-thinking customers if it were to get any traction. As a result, they focused their marketing on the tech sector beginning around 1995.

They were spot on: once they were able to convince a tech company to try it out, the employees found the chair so incredibly comfortable that they didn't care about the aesthetics. In fact, they embraced the look of it—viewing it as a symbol of forward thinking and ingenuity.

After that, the chair's sales took off. It was the height of the dot-com era, and it became such a success that human resource departments began marketing them as an employee benefit to attract highly sought-after tech workers. Sales continued to soar as the dot-com bubble bulged in the late 1990s and even after it crashed in 2000.

Once the chair became a cool product in the tech sector, other industries that wanted to be considered state of the art and forward thinking started buying the chairs to achieve the same cachet. This included companies in much older and more traditional industries such as banking, insurance, and law.

**If no one is adopting an iconoclast's idea right away, it's rarely because it is a bad one. Rather, because it deviates from the norm, most people simply need more time to adapt to it.**

What was once an ugly industry pariah was now considered beautiful and trendy. But nothing had actually changed about it physically. The transformation occurred only in the minds of the masses. This journey is the way of the iconoclast.

What we can draw from the Aeron chair story is that iconoclasts by their very nature see opportunities much earlier than other people. If no one is adopting an iconoclast's idea right away, it's rarely because it is a bad one. Rather, because it deviates from the norm, most people simply need more time to adapt to it.

The book *Crossing the Chasm*, by Geoffrey A. Moore, does a really great job of outlining what is known as the technology adoption lifecycle. It is something that iconoclasts need to be aware of.

**The Chasm**
from *Crossing the Chasm* by Geoffrey A. Moore

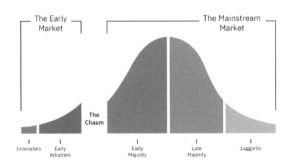

*Geoffrey A. Moore's technology adoption lifecycle, from Crossing the Chasm (HarperCollins, 1991).*

The figure on the previous page appears in Moore's book and illustrates that most change can be charted on a bell curve. To the extreme left of the curve are innovators and early adopters, followed by the early majority—those who are quick to embrace change. On the right are the late majority, followed by the laggards—those who are slow to do so. There is often a drop in adoption rates when crossing from the early adopters to the early majority, hence the title of the book *Crossing the Chasm*. What the curve can't predict, though, is the timeline for change. While the bell curve can cover just a few years for some technologies, full adoption for others may take three decades.

The length of time to reach general acceptance is one factor that can make iconoclasm a lonely road, but if you can hang in there, the potential payoff is tremendous.

# Part 3 Summary and Questions

## CHAPTER SUMMARY

- A drone is someone who does not think for themselves and prefers to let others think for them.

- People become drones out of habit or out of survival, and we are all drones in some areas of our lives.

- Though entrepreneurs, inventors, and philanthropists are often iconoclasts, that's not always the case. Quite simply, iconoclasts challenge the existing paradigm, design a better way, and implement it, whether they are executives, technologists, practitioners, or parents.

- Iconoclasts often have to be patient, as the journey to acceptance in the eyes of the masses typically takes time.

## QUESTIONS TO CONSIDER

- How many times in your life can you recall acting as a drone out of habit? What about out of survival?

- What are the traits of an entrepreneur, inventor, philanthropist, and iconoclast? How do they differ from one another? Where might they overlap?

- Can you recall a time in your life where you felt like you had a solution to a problem but no one understood it? How long did you have to wait for others to catch on?

# PART 4

# ICONOCLASM AND ENTREPRENEURSHIP

This section of the book is designed to help entrepreneurs understand whether or not they are—or want to be—iconoclasts. If you are not thinking about being an entrepreneur, then you can go ahead and skip this section as well as the next section on business financing.

Just so we're all on the same page, let's review our definition of an entrepreneur: "Someone willing to assume risk in a business venture in anticipation of a return on that investment."

With a solid definition on the table, we can drill down into the different types of entrepreneurs. We've established that many—but not all—entrepreneurs are iconoclasts. Why? There are different types of entrepreneurs, just as there are different types of leaders.

Understanding which type of entrepreneur you are is key to helping you form a strategy for success. It can help you determine how to effectively grow your organization and your skill set.

# The Three Types of Entrepreneurs

As I became an entrepreneur and began expanding my company, it became obvious to me that the business world was crazy. It's easy to get caught up in the potential for growth and shirk one's ethics and purpose in the process. To avoid that, I knew I needed to establish a set of principles to stick to.

There are a lot of ways to grow a business as well, so I also had to figure out which route I wanted to take.

> Knowing what type of entrepreneur you are affects the way you address some of the questions that come with being a business leader.

I did what many new business owners do and talked to other entrepreneurs to figure out what my principles and protocols for growing my business would be. I spoke to hundreds of different entrepreneurs as I charted my path forward. I struck up conversations in formal settings like Young Presidents' Organization chapter meetings, leadership round tables, and advisory panels, as well as informal settings like networking dinners, barbecues, and cocktail parties. Along the way, I learned that there were basically three types of entrepreneurs leading companies:

1. Investor-driven entrepreneurs

2. Innovation-driven entrepreneurs

3. Mission-driven entrepreneurs

Knowing what type of entrepreneur you are affects the way you address some of the questions that come with being a business leader:

- How much of my own money should I invest in the company?

- How much of my own time should I invest in the company?

- What jobs/roles do I want to hold at the company?

- What jobs/roles do I want to delegate?

- How long do I want to actively work at this company?

- How do I want to shape the culture at the company?

- What types of employees do I want to hire?

Further, knowing what type of entrepreneur you are will dictate the decisions you make with regard to the following four areas:

1. Your managerial priorities or prime directives

2. The customer experience and value you aim to provide

3. The employee working conditions and culture you promote

4. Your longevity at the company

We'll lay out the characteristics for each of the three types of entrepreneurs, but let's clarify something first: not all CEOs are entrepreneurs. Some CEOs are just proven managers working for investors. What keeps them squarely in the CEO category? They do not assume a greater-than-normal financial risk.

We can refer to this type of CEO as a "hired gun." A hired gun is *not* financially invested in the company in the same way an entrepreneur would be. In addition, they are likely less emotionally invested in the business as well, since it's probably not their vision they're fulfilling—and they have less at stake when it comes to the business's success. Rather, a hired gun actually represents the interests, vision, and goals of someone else. As such, we're not talking about hired guns in this chapter; they just aren't entrepreneurs.

## INVESTOR-DRIVEN ENTREPRENEUR

Let's start with the first type of entrepreneur, the investor-driven entrepreneur. This type of entrepreneur is not really concerned with the mission of the company, or the product or service it sells. This doesn't mean they don't care about the mission or whether the product is innovative. It just means that those factors don't move them emotionally. The mission and product are just variables in their equation of success.

Most investor-driven entrepreneurs end up as venture capitalists, as that strategy aligns most closely with their own. Their first company simply serves as their first venture. The primary directive for the investor entrepreneur is to sell their ownership stake in the company for a great price, and they will often cash out when they get it.

For better or for worse, the quality of the customer experience is typically linked to the entrepreneur's emotional investment in the company. Unfortunately, the customer experience can be quite horrible when the investor entrepreneur is looking to sell quickly. The entrepreneur may choose to spend a lot of money on marketing to obtain customers quickly without caring about their longevity. Why? Bringing in a lot of customers fast can look like high growth on paper and result in a higher valuation of the company when the investor looks to sell. However, once they are captured, the customers may find that their expectations are not being met or that the service or product they are receiving is actually inferior to that of the operation's competition.

On the other hand, if the investor-driven entrepreneur is not looking to sell immediately, the customer experience can be very good. This is especially the case if the company has a strategy of being the low-cost provider in its industry while offering higher-than-average levels of customer service in their industry. There can be amazing deals for the customer in particular if the company is offering artificially low prices to build market share.

For employees, companies led by investor entrepreneurs are typically not the best places and cultures in which to work. Employee turnover is often high and people are seen as just a means to achieve a high return on investment.

Most investor entrepreneurs do not stay on as CEO for a long period of time, unless they believe doing so is their best investment option over other choices. Investor entrepreneurs who do last a while in a leadership role at their company typically have a very grand "let's dominate the world" agenda and believe they can achieve it. It's not uncommon for the ego of the investor-driven entrepreneur to be the real force behind the organization's growth. What do I mean by this? The thrill and accolades that come with being more successful than their mentor, peers, or even successful historical figures serves as their true source of motivation. Examples of famous investor entrepreneurs include Bill Gates, Warren Buffet, and Jeff Bezos.

## INNOVATION-DRIVEN ENTREPRENEUR

An innovation-driven entrepreneur is really an artist in the form of a businessperson. They are obsessed with how their technology, service, or product can change the marketplace and the world, and fulfilling this vision is their prime directive. They typically take great pride in every detail of their product.

As a customer of an innovation-driven, entrepreneur-led company, you may have a fantastic experience, as the business's leader truly cares what you think of their product. Customers of these companies often form communities around the company to share experiences and bond.

Working for an innovator entrepreneur can be a really fantastic experience if you share the passion for their vision. In that case, you may be considered a family member. An innovator entrepreneur will typically have longevity at their company so long as they can maintain cash flow for the business and increase its profitability over time. An innovator entrepreneur typically does not look to sell their equity in the company unless they see it as necessary to deliver on the mass adoption of their innovation. Henry Ford, Steve Jobs, Elon Musk, and Howard Schultz are all examples of innovation-driven entrepreneurs.

## MISSION-DRIVEN ENTREPRENEURS

Mission-driven entrepreneurs are focused on a primary directive: making their customers' world a better place. Although—like any entrepreneur—they enjoy the prospect of a good return on investment and appreciate a healthy profit margin, this is not the primary reason they go into business. That's one factor that differentiates them from an innovation-driven entrepreneur.

Moreover, unlike the innovation-driven entrepreneur, a missionary entrepreneur will also adopt and drop technologies as needed with the goal of benefiting their customers. The customer is the priority, not their innovation.

Missionary entrepreneurs tend to care about the price of their product or service. Since they want more people to experience the mission, they tend to price their offerings very competitively so more customers can join in.

Companies led by these entrepreneurs tend to be very good places to work because the entrepreneur often recognizes that having good people is critical to their long-term success and customer satisfaction.

Mission-driven companies tend to be privately held, and the entrepreneur running things tends to stay with the company most of their working life. They often take great pride in watching the company grow and consider their business to be an extension of their life's purpose.

> The iconoclast formula will best serve mission-driven entrepreneurs. This is because the iconoclast formula most often transcends both technology and return on investment.

Examples of famous mission-driven entrepreneurs include Michael Dell, S. Truett Cathy, and Herb Kelleher.

How does iconoclasm apply to the three types of entrepreneurs we just discussed? The iconoclast formula will best serve mission-driven entrepreneurs. This is because the iconoclast formula most often transcends both technology and return on investment. It holistically accounts for people's habits and beliefs just as much as the tools they have to operate with. If you are or want to be a mission-driven entrepreneur, this book should be your strategic bible. Pay close attention to the next section on business financing.

The iconoclast formula will serve innovation-driven entrepreneurs as well but not necessarily to the same extent as it will the mission entrepreneur since it is not just about invention and innovative technology. In most cases, it will not be of much use to the investor-driven entrepreneur. If that's you, feel free to skip the next section on financing business growth.

# Financing Business Growth

There are many people who are very intimidated by the barriers to start a business, especially when they consider the money necessary to start a venture, also known as capital. It is very easy for an entrepreneur to become fixated on capital when there are many other obstacles to consider and plan for that can end up being more important and challenging to overcome. The following are examples of potential barriers to market entry:

- Government tax incentives for a competitive offering

- Access to materials

- Patents

- A competitor's strong brand identity

- Proper licenses

- Regulatory clearance

- The cost of educating the market

- The customer cost of switching brands

Still, capital does serve as a barrier to entry in many cases—and it's one people are most concerned about—so let's talk about the challenges it can present.

## CAPITAL AS A BARRIER TO ENTRY

Some business ventures require an initial large investment to start out, depending on the product or service. For example, say you want to build a new hotel in downtown Tampa Bay, Florida. To bring this business plan to life, you would have to put up the capital to build the hotel before you could make your first dollar renting rooms.

The same might be true if you were planning to manufacture a product. Let's say, hypothetically, that your manufacturing process required that you have your own nuclear reactor. Without the reactor, you couldn't begin production. There are no other options, as having your own manufacturing facility—complete with the machinery necessary to run it—is part of your core differentiation in the marketplace. As of this writing, the starting price to secure all the equipment and materials necessary to build a small nuclear reactor is roughly US $25 million.

Another example? Maybe you want to sell the widest variety of wristwatches available with a two-day delivery guarantee. This business model requires you to have $5 million of inventory on hand, as well as a warehouse from which to launch and run the business. All three of these examples would certainly qualify as capital-intensive ventures by most people's standards.

There are several investors that target industries with large capital-based barriers to entry, as these tend to be less competitive than others. In addition, they can earn a higher rate of return on their investment than they would be able to in industries that don't require much capital to enter into the market. Many service-based businesses fall into the latter category. Here are some examples:

- Plumbing companies

- Electrical contracting

- Single-home residential construction

- Management-consulting organizations

- Businesses offering legal advisory and litigation services

- Home-inspection businesses

- Technology-consulting companies

I'm not taking the time to describe capital as a barrier to entry to suggest that you launch a service-based business or drop your dream of entrepreneurship. Rather, I'm covering the subject because it is very common for entrepreneurs to misunderstand why they need capital and how much they must have to launch. A little iconoclastic thinking can help you overcome any misconceptions you may have about how much you actually need to get started. With that in mind, let's break down the idea of capital with iconoclastic thinking using our three-step formula:

## Step 1: Challenge the Existing Way

Start by asking, "Why is it this way, and is there an opportunity to do things differently?"

Most entrepreneurs believe they need a ton of investment money to start a business. They have been led to believe their business won't grow or thrive without substantial seed money. Where does this false assumption come from? Venture capitalists are marketing this story to promote their own self-interest.

The National Venture Capital Association is a policy advisory and research organization that provides quite a bit of data on the venture capital market. According to the NVCA, as of 2019 there are 1,328 venture capital firms in existence, with over $444 billion of investments or assets under management.[6] If you have been in business the last ten years, you've likely seen the extraordinary growth of venture capitalists in the market. The following chart shows the steady growth of VC investments over the past sixteen years, and the trend is only continuing:

---

6    "NVCA 2020 Yearbook," National Venture Capital Association, https://nvca.org/wp-content/uploads/2020/03/NVCA-2020-Yearbook.pdf.

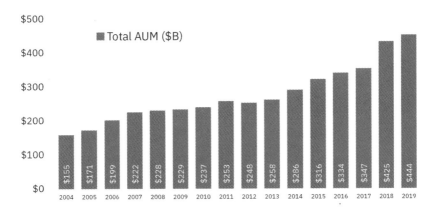

*NVCA 2020 Yearbook. Data provided by PitchBook.*

Venture capitalists are looking for a ten-times return on their initial investment in a seven-to-ten-year time frame. You don't need to do the math to know those numbers are insane. There are some businesses that can produce this kind of result on their own, but many are not capable of achieving such rapid growth in that period of time.

If you are interested in learning more about the venture capital market, I recommend watching the documentary *Something Ventured.* Filmed in 2011, it features venture capitalists Arthur Rock, Tom Perkins, Don Valentine, Dick Kramlich, Reid Dennis, Bill Draper, Pitch Johnson, Bill Bowes, Bill Edwards, and Jim Gaither.

The documentary makes clear that venture capital can be a noble profession and has its place in the world. However, it should be reserved for really big, capital-intensive opportunities that are going to reshape the way we live and deliver an enormous ten-times return on investments. The documentary features the stories of companies like Intel, Atari, Genentech, Apple, and Cisco.

While early venture capitalist firms in the 1960s and 1970s provided a high-risk, high- reward opportunity to entrepreneurs, the idea to make this kind of money caught on as a cool business model for firms without such noble ambitions. There is unfortunately a dark side of the venture capital market. Having talked to hundreds of entrepreneurs over the past twenty-five years, I have heard the story many times over, and it goes something like this:

1. An entrepreneur believes in their vision of changing the world and establishes a company to achieve it.

2. A venture capitalist sees a valid business that can grow quickly and exponentially.

3. The VC makes a large investment to take controlling interest of the company.

4. The VC firm pumps twenty times the existing budget of the firm into marketing and hires an expensive management team they have worked with in the past to take over the managerial relationships.

5. In twenty-four to twenty-six months, the company does not meet its insane sales goals, and the founder of the company is blamed for its poor performance.

6. The VC firm fires the founder, takes control of the company, and sells the business to another investment firm at a premium.

Venture capital unfortunately has those bad actors who are really just interested in corporate takeovers. And whether a venture capital firm is good or bad, the VCs have had to increase their marketing spend to attract the companies they want to invest in. As a result, they have to tell a story that you've likely become familiar with: that you need serious capital to start a business and that VCs are the best people and organizations from which to get it. Thus, the internet, business conferences, and social media platforms are flooded with this message. Since noble and crooked VCs alike benefit from the same marketing story, both contribute to its proliferation.

The truth is, you can start a business from nothing, and you can do it without taking outside capital. I did so myself. It does require that you have a vision of how you want to grow, as well as a high level of adaptability.

You have to start small, and know that you may end up smaller than you imagine. However, achieving steady and healthy growth, the kind that allows you to maintain control of the company and stay true to your mission, provides a good life. It's just not the life that necessarily secures big headlines in the media.

Plus, the reality is that more financing options have become available to small businesses in the last ten years, as has the recognition that VC firms employ the marketing tactic we just discussed to attract fledgling companies.

The traditional lending market for banking has opened up many more options for software and service businesses. In 2019 I was able to get a substantial line of credit from my bank that covered my operating expenses for roughly two and a half months, which helped us immensely in taking more calculated risks while we grow. I have also spoken to many other service-based companies who were able to secure the same type of instrument.

For example, Lighter Capital is an alternative financing company focused on the technology space that issues loans against a business's recurring revenue base. Its model represents the kind of nontraditional financing that really works for many companies. The bottom line is outside capital isn't necessary for a company to achieve success over time.

## Step 2: Make a Plan

Many businesses in both manufacturing and services can start without a large capital investment. Plan to start smaller, own your business, and grow with it. Determine the resources you'll need and how you'll acquire and deploy them to bring your vision to life.

## Step 3: Execute a Plan

For many, the first step to successful entrepreneurship is figuring out a way to jailbreak themselves from their current day job. The plan won't go very far so long as it is a side hustle. That may mean putting in nights and weekends up front to build up the resources to leave.

Once you are able to employ yourself full time, the business will grow, and you can hire people to fulfill roles as required. In the meantime, you can depend on contract services when you can't justify the expense of a full-time employee. Repeat this process as you grow.

With an iconoclastic approach, you'll see your options increase—even as the business world continues to embrace more limited opportunities and narratives, like the one VCs provide. Remember that the iconoclast way often looks weird, sounds crazy, and receives a lot of doubt from others in the beginning. It is nontraditional by definition, so others will naturally be uncomfortable with it at first. But therein lies its potential.

# Part 4 Summary and Questions

## CHAPTER SUMMARY

- There are three primary types of entrepreneurs: investor-driven entrepreneurs, innovation-driven entrepreneurs, and mission-driven entrepreneurs.

- Some are more suited to iconoclasm than others.

- Outside capital is not needed as much as we have been led to believe when starting a business—particularly if one chooses to harness the iconoclast formula.

## QUESTIONS TO CONSIDER

- Do you consider yourself an entrepreneur? If so, which type?

- Are you struggling with a financial plan to start a business? You may want to try applying the iconoclast formula to identify and pursue a better way.

# PART 5

# HOW I BECAME AN ICONOCLAST

By now, you may have noticed that a big chunk of this book focuses on my personal story and how I became an iconoclast. You might be saying to yourself, "I don't care about *your* personal story because it doesn't relate to *me* and my experience to date." But the reality is that concrete examples serve as powerful teaching tools—particularly when the subject matter is highly complex. It is far easier to grasp a concept by looking at the specific path of a person or an organization, rather than an abstract theory.

If you're doubting the value of this approach, we can turn to Harvard Business School. Harvard Business School has been the number one business school in the country for many, many years. Its primary subjects—business management, strategy, and entrepreneurship—are very difficult to teach. There are several people, even in the academic world, who say entrepreneurship actually can't be taught; you're either born with an entrepreneurial spirit or you're not.

With that said, if you look at how Harvard teaches business, it's mostly through case studies. In addition to teaching the theories behind business topics, professors present numerous case studies on organizations that have struggled or achieved success based on a certain principle. These case studies compose a large portion of the curriculum because they are such an effective means of conveying concepts.

> To be an iconoclast—a role that comes with its own complexities—it pays to study and understand other people's journeys and apply what you have learned from them to your unique circumstances.

To be an iconoclast—a role that comes with its own complexities—it pays to study and understand other people's journeys and apply what you have learned from them to your unique circumstances. That's why I'm sharing my story, including the successes and professional and personal struggles I've encountered along the way. It's a case study in iconoclasm, one I hope you'll benefit from.

## The Foundation of Gymnastics— and Iconoclasm

I grew up in the town of Hinsdale, in the state of Illinois. Hinsdale is a fairly affluent town in the west suburbs of Chicago. My family did not fit too well into our community socially, as we were very much lower middle class. My mother was a stay-at-home parent caring for three children, and my father was an IT administrator at a manufacturing company.

I spent my entire childhood in Hinsdale, graduating from Hinsdale Central High School in 1992. During my time in Hinsdale, it was not at all what you would call a multicultural village. The population at the time was probably about 95 percent white. Despite its cultural shortcomings, the school had a lot of resources and a wonderful athletic program at the high school level. We excelled in what people referred to as "country club" sports: swimming, tennis, and golf.

I have always been very strong physically—though I'm pretty short for a guy at just five feet, seven inches. In elementary school, it became very obvious that I did not have the right body type to be successful at football or basketball. So I tried a wide variety of sports, including baseball, soccer, skiing, wrestling, and gymnastics. With my particular build—strong and short—it soon became clear that I was ideally built for three sports in particular: weight lifting, wrestling, and gymnastics.

Since my high school did not have a weight lifting team, I started settling into wrestling and gymnastics, but I knew I'd ultimately have to choose one. Given the tremendous differences in the training regimens involved in each sport, I knew I couldn't be a champion in both. At the end of the day, I was just enamored with the strength, agility, and cool tricks gymnastics had to offer.

I think my fascination with gymnastics actually began long before I was introduced to the sport, when I saw Luke Skywalker do a backflip to escape from Darth Vader during a light-saber battle in *Return of the Jedi*. I was also heavily influenced by the 1984 Olympics, during which the US men's gymnastics team won the gold medal. That was the year the Soviet Union boycotted the Olympics; nonetheless we had a very impressive team, featuring Bart Conner, Tim Daggett, Mitch Gaylord, Jim Hartung, Scott Johnson, Peter Vidmar, and Jim Mikus (alternate).

Witnessing some of the older guys do backflips and elaborate tricks in the gymnastics facility where I took classes only impressed me further. I decided being a gymnast would give me an arsenal of party tricks to impress girls, and at age fourteen, I couldn't think of anything more valuable than that! I decided gymnastics was the right sport for me when I entered my freshman year of high school in 1988.

Once I committed to gymnastics, I got addicted to it pretty quickly. Nowadays there are quite a few types of gymnastics out there. I competed in what is now referred to as "men's artistic gymnastics." In men's artistic gymnastics, which is still my favorite event to watch in the Olympics, there are actually six apparatuses and seven events for competition. The six apparatuses are the floor exercise, pommel horse, still rings, vault, parallel bars, and high bar. The seventh event in the sport is called the all-around. The all-around is a competition in which you combine all six of the scores for each apparatus into one total score. The winning all-arounder is the person who can get the highest score when totaling the individual scores for all six apparatus events.

When I started training as a gymnast, it was obvious I was getting stronger and more agile as each week passed. I did enjoy this increase in athletic performance; however, it wasn't the factor that made me truly adore the sport. I fell in love with gymnastics because it combined three primary elements—creativity, engineering, and discipline—that would also later become essential in my journey to iconoclasm.

## LEARNING CREATIVITY

Let's talk about creativity first. At the time, each gymnast would make up their own routine on each apparatus. A routine consisted of about eleven moves or tricks performed in a sequence. The tricks were rated by difficulty, on a scale from A to E. An A-rated trick was the easiest, while an E-rated trick was the hardest. When I was competing, the sport was judged on a scale from zero to ten. The more difficult the tricks in your routine, the higher you could score—and the closer you could get to that perfect ten. A routine had to have at least four B moves and one C move to achieve a high score in the nines.

The highest rewards in gymnastics come from creativity. If you create a new trick in gymnastics, it becomes your namesake—at least for a while, meaning anyone around the world who performs that trick references your name. (By the way, in this day and age it is insanely hard to invent a new trick in gymnastics.) You also get to choose your routine, including the tricks you perform and the sequence in which you perform them. The ones chosen largely depend on individual strengths, whether that's flexibility, balance, or particularly strong shoulders or legs.

When I was competing, judges were always very impressed with creativity—the willingness and desire to do something different. It is the creativity element that makes this sport so special. With the exception of figure skating, there are very few other sports that provide the opportunity to incorporate creativity as part of its core operations. Sports like baseball, soccer, basketball, tennis, and skiing involve strategy but not much creativity. In football, we see some creativity with different plays—but the amount needed pales in comparison to gymnastics. I started taking age-group gymnastics when I was in seventh grade. So at a fairly early age, I was working hard to be creative and learning how to do it well—a skill that would be incredibly valuable as I entered the business world.

## LEARNING ENGINEERING

Once you decide what your routine will be as a gymnast, you typically have to present it to your coach. Most of the time, routines are decided about three months prior to the competition season. While gymnastics is somewhat of a year-round sport, high school and college seasons tend to run from February to May.

The summer is spent trying new tricks and attempting to up the difficulty of your return. But as the fall and winter approach, it's time to establish that routine and get the coach's approval. Why the long time frame? Perfecting that routine requires a lot of engineering.

Success in gymnastics, like a lot of things, is a numbers game. A gymnast knows if they try a trick enough times and they have the proper coaching and technique, they should be able to get it eventually—so long as the trick is in their skill range. For example, say I wanted to perform a round-off, back handspring, double back on the floor exercise, and it was within my ability to do so. Let's further assume that I would need to perform the sequence on its own ten times successfully before I could put it into a routine. And then let's say if I wanted to execute my routine without any flaws in competition by the second week of February, I would need to perform the whole routine without any flaws ten times in a row prior to the first competition.

Once I establish those benchmarks, I can reverse engineer a plan to master all the tricks in my routine, and for all the routines I'll need to develop prior to the competition. I can reverse engineer a set of goals to achieve the outcome I'm looking for in each routine. And then I can break down the goals I've established to determine what needs to be done on a weekly or daily basis. As an all-arounder, I kept a note card listing all the tricks and sequences I planned to do for each event. Every day, I'd train on two or three events and plan and track my goals accordingly.

It was amazing how well I could engineer a plan for success when I accounted for all the variables out there, including my timeline. Engineering workouts was certainly a skill, and the more I performed as a gymnast, knew my body, and the skills I wanted to master, the easier the engineering became.

In hindsight, with my competition training program in gymnastics, I really embraced the agile methodology. Agile is a work methodology in the software in which one produces an improved, distributable version of one's product every two to three weeks. Every two weeks, I had deliverables and created a product in the form of a routine. I would then try to improve that routine, making small changes and additions to up its difficulty—skills that would eventually serve me as an iconoclast.

## LEARNING DISCIPLINE

Now that you've seen that gymnastics has elements of creativity and engineering, let me describe the discipline required. One may find the creativity and engineering inherent in gymnastics to be the fun and easy parts of being a gymnast, as they don't require physical effort. It is the discipline of stretching the body, working the daily tricks, and conditioning for strength that makes winners in gymnastics— but that discipline often poses the greatest challenge. It is a lot of physical work to train at an elite level. From my sophomore through senior years in high school, I often trained four hours a day, six days a week. I loved almost every minute of it. I also had wonderful coaches that I will be forever grateful for. Thank you, Hinsdale Central gymnastics coaches Neil Krupicka, Mark Wanner, and Myles Laffey, for coaching me!

I did fairly well as a gymnast. My senior year, I was Illinois state champion on the still rings, and I got second place on the vault. I was also one of just a few gymnasts in the history of the state to make it to the state competition finals in all six apparatus events that year.

I had no idea at the time that the sport of gymnastics would lay the foundation of what I would become later in life, an iconoclast. But now I realize that gymnastics is completely analogous to the life of an iconoclast. The creativity of forming one's own routine serves as a direct parallel to the creative thinking one does as an iconoclast, challenging the existing paradigm and asking if there's another way. The engineering one does in creating a training schedule is identical to engineering a plan in business—or really in any area in which there are deliverables and a timeline. And the discipline required to physically execute the training routine corresponds directly to the discipline to execute any plan one forms as an iconoclast.

When you experience success in a sport like gymnastics, that achievement becomes very addictive. Improving your routines as a gymnast is really just a form of leveling up, as routines are typically improved just a little bit at a time. A gymnast will swap out a B-rated trick for a C-rated trick or trade two A-rated tricks for one B-rated move in the same routine. It's not unusual to see gymnasts simply upgrade their routines over the years by replacing easier moves with harder ones within a similar structure.

Focusing on incremental improvement is a foundational trait necessary to be an iconoclast and/or level up. Doing so allows you to hold on to what you have while improving step by step, rather than aiming to achieve major progress all at once. Looking back, it was improving incrementally that made me love the sport of gymnastics so much.

# Finding My Profession

Like many young adults, I had to find myself—and my profession. If there was any time in my life that I felt lost in terms of direction, it was my twenties. Coming out of college, the world just seemed so enormous, complex, and overwhelming. Looking back on these years, I didn't feel like I had the confidence to be an iconoclast. I was just too busy trying to figure out how the world worked.

Unfortunately, I was a relatively normal college kid—a clear-cut case of "youth being wasted on the young"! I formed a habit in school of simply memorizing facts and equations, regurgitating them on my exams, and then mass deleting them from my brain on the way to the house party or bar after finals. I was the rule, not the exception—and I was even considered a good student. I had a high GPA and was summa cum laude. But I did not internalize much of my education. I did not process what I was learning in my courses or think about its context.

Instead, I figured that life as a student was pretty simple. You studied the material and took the test. Every problem or challenge had a solution. However, I would learn that life in the real world required me to use my brain and figure things out. Every problem had a variety of approaches with different potential outcomes. I could have used those courses to prepare—to question what I had been absorbing in my classes and consider a different way. Here I was being prepared to take on society as an adult, and I blew the opportunity! Looking back on college, I am not sure I learned much of anything.

With my experience in mind, I must say that, to this day, I don't put a lot of stock in academic credentials. Courses are necessary and help us learn the theory behind some of our professional tasks, and they can help us move up in the world, but it is always real-world experience that counts most.

## UNCOVERING SOME ANSWERS IN ACCOUNTING

I have a sister, Angela, who is four years older than me. She graduated from college in 1992 and came back home to live with the family just as I was setting off on my own college career, but I would see her on breaks and in between semesters. The US economy had hit a recession in 1990, which continued on through the early nineties. Each time I returned, I watched Angela and all her friends struggle to find jobs. With their experience in mind, I decided that I needed to pick a college major that had good employment potential post-graduation. School had never been for me, and I couldn't wait to get out into the real world and get paid for my hard work, rather than reaping the completely underwhelming reward of a report card twice a year.

Of all subjects that I had learned about in school, I just loved business. And while I didn't enjoy school, I loved all my classes on business—including those in marketing, management, and sales. However, when it came to job placement stats, accounting crushed all these majors. All the major CPA firms came to campus and recruited their new workers right from buildings where I was taking my classes. You didn't even have to search for a job—that job would find you! Fortunately, I found accounting very interesting and practical. What fun it is to count your money and determine what you have financially! Majoring in accounting was a no-brainer as far as I was concerned.

So I made the commitment to accounting and studied hard. I didn't even have to wait until school was done to search for a job. In the fall of 1995, BDO, one of the largest international public accounting firms in the world, made me an offer right out of school. I would be an audit associate in their Grand Rapids, Michigan, office starting in July of 1996. My plan worked well and paid off—so it seemed, at least.

I was about a year into my job at BDO when I began to understand why public accounting jobs paid well and were always in demand. It is because the work is so utterly boring. What I loved about business was the creativity, the challenge of dominating a market segment, the opportunity to be innovative. But being a certified public accountant (CPA) was really more like being an attorney than a businessperson—one who never got to have their day in court.

I was bored to tears combing through companies' books well after life had happened and making sure they were in compliance with generally accepted accounting principles. About one year into my time at BDO, I made a plan to finish a full two years there and become a CPA, since I had invested so much into being an accountant already.

In Michigan at the time, you needed to have two years of experience working in a public accounting firm and to pass the CPA exam to earn the CPA certificate. Preparing for the CPA exam was essentially a sequel to my college experience, in which I studied hard, locked facts into my short-term memory to pass the exam, and let most of it go afterward. There was even a long-standing joke among the office associates that if you got a score higher than a seventy-five, the minimum you needed to pass, you had wasted your time studying too much.

Once I reached the two-year mark, I decided to go work for other companies as an accountant and try to work my way up the corporate ladder to become a chief financial officer. That seemed to align much more closely with what I was after. In that role, I'd be part of a company's business team, being innovative and driving its growth and success. That sounded a lot like being a gymnast. It required creativity and engineering.

Though I was ready for a different challenge, looking back I am so thankful for my experience at BDO. It was a fantastic company to work for. The firm was innovative, provided great learning opportunities, and took great care of its employees. I have a ton of respect for my fellow public accountants, and the experience I obtained as I earned my CPA certificate has been invaluable to me.

## EVALUATING BUSINESS SCHOOL

Based on my longtime love of business and my desire to make more money, I was intrigued by the idea of going to business school after becoming a CPA. I started looking into different programs and researching what was involved in taking the GMAT. And I also did something else: I started applying the iconoclast formula to the decision in front of me. I first asked myself a series of questions:

- Why do business schools exist?

- Why do people decide to attend business school?

- Who should be going to business school?

- Is anyone telling me I need to go to business school? If so, who?

- Is business school something that will allow me to truly advance in my career?

As I was researching my options, it became very apparent to me that there were three career tracks that really benefited from a business school education: finance, management consulting, and business management for engineers.

I came to this conclusion by looking at the average salary for business school graduates. I focused specifically on those who had attended the top ten business schools in the United States. When I looked at the situation from a pure ROI perspective, these were the only three career tracks in which individuals earned significantly higher salaries after graduating from business school, meaning there was only a real return on investment of your time, lost wages, and tuition for these three career paths.

As a result I had to ask myself, Do I want a career in finance? Do I want a career in management consulting? The third category simply did not apply to me: it's for those with engineering or technology backgrounds who want to move into a management role within a company. It seems to be the most traditional track for business school, and I still think it is a very valid one. The reality was that I was not interested in any of these career tracks. I wanted to start a business and be an entrepreneur.

As a result, I decided to skip business school altogether and just keep focusing on entrepreneurial ideas and trying to develop them. This also seemed like sound logic, as at the time the loudest voices telling me I needed to go to business school were the business schools themselves. Business schools spend a lot of money on marketing to their target population, just like any other organization. They place an abundance of advertisements in publications like *Forbes*, *Fortune*, and the *Wall Street Journal*. Through these ads, they rope young professionals like myself into thinking they need one of them.

But when I actually talked to the companies hiring people for business-based roles, very few of them cared if you had a business school degree, even for most of the management positions they were working to fill. It was largely previous experience and one's track record as a manager that served as criteria in their hiring or promotion decisions.

Meanwhile, business schools have created a paradigm that young professionals need their schools to effectively progress professionally. I know so many people who went to business school and don't use their degrees whatsoever. Many of them think in hindsight it was mostly a waste of time. This is why it's so important to challenge why you're feeling the way you do when analyzing the prescribed way. In this case, you cannot overlook the marketing impact of the schools themselves on your opinion of them. Why? Because business schools have an economic interest in creating and fostering the notion that many young professionals need their services, when only a small subset really do.

## Finding My Passion and Challenging a Paradigm

From 1998 to 2005, I worked as an accountant in several roles at three different companies. I was a controller and internal auditor and then worked my way up the ladder in management to be pretty close to that CFO position. In 2005, I did a lot of reflecting on my career and what made me happy at work. I had noticed a trend: the days when I enjoyed work the most were the ones I spent learning and playing with software to manage all the accounting data.

I had come to the conclusion that I liked being an accountant for companies, but what I really loved was engineering the software technology used to automate the accounting. I actually loved learning about the technology stacks and programming languages as tools to streamline, engineer, and automate the work accountants typically do more than I liked the activity of managing and reconciling the accounting data itself. In fact I really didn't like managing and reconciling the accounting data at all, and I wanted to employ more software and tools to streamline my accounting job in any way I could.

With that in mind, I decided to change career tracks and get a job as an enterprise resource planning (ERP) computer systems consultant. I started consulting on the ERP systems I had used at the companies I had worked with as an accountant.

In 2008, I decided to start my own business consulting on back-office ERP systems. I had always wanted to be an entrepreneur, and the demand for my skills was quite high. There was plenty of work to be done in the Baltimore-Washington, DC, corridor where I had relocated in 2003 for my last accounting job.

I consulted primarily on three ERP products: Microsoft Dynamics SL and GP and SAP Business One. These products serviced midsize businesses—organizations with revenues between US $2 million and US $100 million and typically with between twenty-five and five thousand employees. Though the Microsoft products were pretty old even back in 2008, they sold very well—after all, accountants typically aren't the types of people who want cutting-edge technology. The accounting mindset embraces caution. Many accountants are risk averse and are considered late adopters when it comes to the technology adoption lifecycle that is outlined in books like *Crossing the Chasm.*

The products I tended to consult on were created with a common paradigm in mind, which we'll refer to as the ERP paradigm. It's summed up in the following statement: "We, the software maker, understand your operating process and technology better than you do. You should adopt our technology and change the way you operate your business if necessary to align with our product."

Of course, this is not a quote from a software maker. But it reflects how the products are manufactured—not how they are marketed. Naturally, the companies all market their products as being state of the art, designed well, reliable, and innovative.

The fact that all these products were built and operated in virtually the same way was something I simply never thought to be odd. In fact, from an accounting technology perspective, it made sense that they fit the status quo. Since I started working with these products early on in my career, it just seemed to make sense that they were all engineered a certain way.

What differentiated one from the next were their preprogrammed functions. Functions in software programs are also called features or routines. A function is just computer code that processes data, typically in the form of creating new data records, reports, or alerts to users.

While one product had functions that processed sales invoices the way most law firms bill their clients, another product would have features written to perform invoicing the way a construction company commonly does it or in a manner in accordance with a medical practice's system or a media company's and so forth.

Software in the midmarket is commonly made for and marketed to customers in a specific industry. It is purpose built and can't be changed much at all. As such, as an ERP consultant, my job really became an exercise of listening to my clients' software requirements and recommending and implementing an ERP system with preprogrammed functions that best matched the way they ran their business already. I would then go on-site at the company's office and work with the employees to start altering their business process to better align with those preprogrammed functions.

When the company's process was too unique for the preprogrammed ERP functions, they would need custom functions. Programming custom functions in the traditional ERP world was a herculean effort. You needed a lot of skill as a developer to do this type of work, and even then it took a lot of time to set up and test the custom data tables, data fields, and processing logic. All that time and effort cost a lot of money, so big budgets were required to go down this path. Only the larger, wealthier organizations could afford this route.

For years, I didn't question the ERP paradigm. Why would I think software could be adapted or changed to fit a company's unique operating processes? I'd never really seen a technology stack do that, despite having worked with dozens of products over the course of my career.

That is, until I came across Salesforce.com.

Around 2008 or 2009, I had a series of customers come to me, all with the same problem. I'd implemented Microsoft midmarket systems for most of them. During the implementation process, I had gained their trust and learned about their businesses quite a bit. I even developed relationships with several of the C-level executives at the companies. Then, all of them came back to me with the same request. My conversations with the CFO or chief information officer at each one went something like this:

CFO: "Tony, we have just implemented Salesforce for quoting and contracting, and it doesn't talk to Microsoft Dynamics—can you integrate these two applications for us?"

Me: "Thanks for considering me for this project, but unfortunately I can't do that. I don't know anything about Salesforce."

CFO: "OK, I understand, but we are having a hard time finding anyone who knows both of these systems."

Me: "Sorry to hear that. I will keep my eye out for someone who does, and let you know if I find them."

About six to eight weeks would go by, and then I'd get another call from the executive. The conversation went basically the same way with all of them:

CFO: "Hey, Tony, we still haven't found anyone who can help us with the Salesforce integration. Can you do it for us?"

Me: "OK, I'll give it a try, but you'll have to pay me to learn this Salesforce platform. As long as you are OK with that, I'm happy to help."

CFO: "We're gonna have to pay somebody. At least you know how the back office works. That makes you the best candidate for the job."

As I got into the Salesforce.com technology stack, I was astonished by what I found. The technology was so far advanced compared to my Microsoft products. It was absolutely mind-blowing how far ahead it was. Salesforce could be customized to fit the customer's needs with just some clicks of the mouse. I didn't really even need to code anything! I could add a custom data table, custom data fields, change the whole interface, and even write simple triggers based on events without having to get a programmer involved at any level.

In my traditional ERP products, all these activities required a ton of effort and skill to complete, requiring the insight of a pretty senior programmer. The deeper I got into Salesforce, the more I could change and alter all aspects of the application effortlessly. Needless to say, I was really mesmerized with this new technology.

The more I studied it, the more I became enamored with the fact that it was essentially a comprehensive tool set to create software that molded to fit anyone's business needs. It also allowed other people to build in their own layers of custom code and data tables if they so chose. Even crazier, other people could layer their customizations on top of mine, as well as Salesforce's core functions, and all of it would work fine together! This was a revolution of the mind! I had never seen anything like it. It was beautiful—and it was a clear demonstration of iconoclast thinking.

Just to make that clear, let's compare the two paradigms at hand.

## THE ERP PARADIGM

"We, the software maker, understand your operating process and technology better than you. You should adopt our technology and change the way you operate your business to align with our technology."

## THE SALESFORCE PARADIGM

"You, the customer, have a unique way of running your business. Here is a set of software tools that you can use to build a data model, user interface, and features that match the way your operating process works or the way you want it to work."

By 2008, I had already consulted with hundreds of companies in my career with regards to IT systems. I was fully aware that no two businesses are really the same in terms of how they operate. It was clear as day that the Salesforce approach was truly the future of software when it came to business management systems.

Products like Salesforce, which give every customer using it the option to customize virtually every aspect of it, use what I call "the snowflake model." The snowflake model is a term used to describe a business model in which every customer can use a particular product in a different way. The uses can all be unique, just as snowflakes are.

## ACCEPTING THE INTEGRATION CHALLENGE

While I was enamored with the Salesforce platform, I had to focus on the projects I had been hired to do: six integrations from Salesforce to Microsoft Dynamics. And it was going to be a challenge. To understand why IT system integrations like these are so difficult to engineer, let me explain how they work.

Pictures are typically much easier to follow than words, so I've drawn you a little diagram.

When you are tracking leads, quotes, and contracts in a CRM system like Salesforce and tracking your accounting in a system like Microsoft, you have to sync, or replicate, a ton of data between the two systems on a constant basis.

Imagine that in front of you there are two databases, which I've drawn as cans. The left can is labeled CRM, which represents Salesforce in this case. The right can is labeled ERP, which represents Microsoft. In the CRM, you are doing lead management, quoting, and contracting. In the ERP, you are billing your customers in accordance with the quotes and contracts you issued out of the CRM system.

In operating both a CRM and an ERP system, you have two different types of data that need to be synchronized between the two applications: master data and transactional data. Master data is foundational data that is used in transactional data. For example, the customer name, billing contact or names, and the products used in quotes are all considered master data records. Transactional data is used to record the actual events that took place between the business and the customer. Giving a quote, signing a contract, or sending an invoice to a customer would all be functions that would be stored in transactional data records.

Now visualize these two cans—the CRM and the ERP—on your right and left side, respectively. The big challenge is that every time you update the master data in one system, it needs to be updated in the other simultaneously or else the databases become out of sync. By the same token, transactional data typically needs to be replicated between the systems to make sure all the business processes have been completed accurately. For example, if you send out a contract in one system, you need all the billing information inside that system to make sure it was billed correctly, or vice versa.

In addition, transactional data depends on master data records to be accurate. Let's say you want to insert a transactional data record into one of the databases, but the master data it depends on does not exist. If this is the case, then the record will not insert—instead it will fail. In fact, there are so many ways for the databases to be out of sync that it's nearly impossible to keep both systems aligned at any one time.

## THE TRADITIONAL SOLUTIONS

There are two basic approaches to trying to keep these databases in sync. One is using a type of software called middleware. Middleware is also known as ETL software. ETL stands for "extract, transform, and load." Middleware serves as a third database in between the two databases that runs a programmed routine on a timer—perhaps every fifteen minutes or twice a day—that searches each database for new records and attempts to update the other database, and vice versa. These tools are a nightmare to manage and rarely work properly.

The second way to try and sync these databases is through API calls. API stands for application programming interface, and it's just a fancy term for a computer talking to another computer over the internet. While a user interface, or UI, is the way a human being sees a computer program, an API is simply the way a computer sees another computer.

To keep these databases in sync with API calls, you need to employ what are called triggers that look for data being updated in one system and then send what is essentially a phone call over to the other system to update the other database. Just as phone calls can be dropped on your cell phone when you are trying to talk to someone and have a bad connection, computers experience the same issue when they are talking to one another over the internet.

As you can see, these two options are highly unreliable and fraught with error. When they fail, which often happens, you have to reconcile them. Reconciling the data between these two systems means running reports out of each application and comparing the results to make sure all the master and transactional data are in both. As you can imagine, this is basically an impossible task for almost any size company to complete.

As a result, most companies give up on the systems actually working together correctly. They will just declare one database to be the pure truth and try to true up the second database periodically—typically once a week, month, or quarter. The bottom line is this type of arrangement costs companies a lot of money, as integrating and reconciling the databases are both expensive tasks.

## SYNCHING SALESFORCE TO OTHER ACCOUNTING PROGRAMS

To fulfill the project work I was contracted to do for each of my six customers, I employed different flavors of the middleware and API approaches. I actually got Salesforce and Microsoft talking to each other. However, all the customers came back to me pretty unhappy with the results. They said that it was impossible to keep these databases in sync and no one ever knew which system was right at any given time. Plus, they were spending a lot of time and money reconciling the systems by constantly running reports and auditing the data. I knew there had to be a different option.

With that realization, we can leave behind the IT nerd stuff—thanks for bearing with me—and talk about what came next.

## An Iconoclast Is Born

There were essentially two factors that prompted me to build an accounting product on the Salesforce platform. The first is that integrating Salesforce with other apps really sucked, to put it bluntly. This phenomenon is not really a reflection on Salesforce but more on the applications one would try to integrate with it. The second factor was passion. I was absolutely enamored with the concept of building a business management software tool set. It felt like playing with Legos or *Minecraft*, two things I love to do.

I became convinced that I needed to bring my idea to the back office. I subsequently contacted Salesforce and executed a partnership agreement to build an accounting system on their platform. Once I had that agreement, I started working nights and weekends building this product and decided to take on two partners to help me code the product and run what was now quickly evolving into a business. I named the business Accounting Seed.

I was able to launch the first version of the Accounting Seed product in July of 2011. The customers came pretty quickly. It wasn't hard to compete against large integration projects that relied on old-school connectors. When people understood my product, they were attracted to it immediately from a technology point of view. Most of my early adopters really grasped the value of the Salesforce platform, so it was a no-brainer for them to take on a product like mine.

It wasn't until a few years later that I noticed a profound pattern. Every time I got on the phone with someone who did not understand the Salesforce technology, I had pretty much the same conversation with them. They all wanted me to show them how my software was built so they could evaluate whether it would work for them. It was in having these conversations—and explaining my approach—that I believe I truly became an iconoclast.

Accounting Seed has more than one thousand customers as of this writing. To get to those thousand customers, I had to talk to representatives from about eleven thousand companies. I probably talked to at least eight thousand of them personally since I didn't have a sales team in the early days. Why am I sharing these numbers? You can see that I ended up repeating myself quite a lot.

Thousands of individuals wanted me to show them how my software worked. Each of them entered the conversation believing it operated the same way as the other platforms they'd used their whole careers. Why would my software be any different? That was the long-standing paradigm they were working with.

As a result, rather than looking for something that was entirely different—something that would align with their business model—they were searching for a product that simply worked with their current business structure. If it did, they would consider purchasing it. If not, they would move on to find one more in line with their operation.

Many of them were surprised by the question I asked on each call: "Tell me what you want your process to be rather than how it works now."

Most of these prospective customers would respond with utter confusion—even annoyance. "Why would I bother telling you how I want it to be? Why don't you just tell me how your software works, and I'll see if it'll work for me?"

In the software world, we're selling somewhat of an invisible product. So the concept of customization can be very difficult for people to grasp.

I'd respond, "*No.* Tell me what you want your process to be. My software will bend to it. It will become the kind of program you need. It is built on a new paradigm. The software is essentially a tool set to be used in the way you want."

They simply didn't know that was available in this modern age of technology and in the platform I was bringing to the marketplace. What I was selling was a technology breakthrough, but they were not aware of what it meant and how they could use it. I had to figure out how to convey that to them. Asking this question over and over again, and responding to customers' concerns, allowed me to effectively challenge how they thought about accounting, ERP, and business management.

> The world keeps changing, and new tools are being formed to help us do our jobs better in every aspect of our lives.

This scenario is so true of almost anything in life. The world keeps changing, and new tools are being formed to help us do our jobs better in every aspect of our lives. But education is crucial, as without it, we just keep doing what we've always done.

By now, I have asked so many people so many times why they do things the way they do them. It has become a habit, in multiple areas of my life. Today, I question others, and—perhaps more importantly—I question myself.

When I really thought about it, I had so many preexisting ideas of how things were supposed to work in numerous areas of my life. I realized so much could be gained by asking why. Each time I did, I seemed to uncover a new opportunity to do something different, something that would improve my professional life—and my personal life.

## Iconoclasm's Personal Applications

Being an iconoclast is not something that necessarily makes a person good. Iconoclasts aren't automatically noble. Rather, iconoclasts can use their skills to do good for others and for society as a whole, or they can do the opposite. I have not always sowed good as an iconoclast and have most definitely used the formula to do the wrong thing at times. Today, I believe my life's purpose is to serve God and my fellow earthly brothers and sisters—but I did not always feel that way.

On April 15, 2012, at the age of thirty-eight, I decided to accept Jesus Christ as my lord and savior and truly try to trust God. That day, I decided to give faith a chance rather than live in fear and rely on my own skills and resources to make my way through the world. I started tithing, or giving 10 percent of my income to my church. I remember crying as I wrote out the checks for the first couple of months. Honestly, at first I just felt like a fool throwing my hard-earned money away. I had no idea that what I was actually doing was starting a new life, one that would not even resemble the old life I had. When I gave faith a chance, it grew and grew. And it continues to grow to this day, as I see God creating opportunities and making miracles in my life all the time.

Every day, after I drive to work and park at the office, I say a prayer before getting out of the car. I pray, "Lord, I am your humble servant, and if it be your will, please help me glorify you through this business, help me serve my earthly brothers and sisters and provide opportunities for my partners and employees. Lord, if you want me to sell this business and do something else with the money in your name, I will do so. I just need you to tell me what to do." I'm always listening for a response.

It's a far cry from how I used to think and live. Prior to April of 2012, I did not always conduct my life in a way that honored God. I thought mostly of myself and lived life in a way that served me primarily. I looked for what is referred to as a win-win deal, which often does create success—but the motivation is typically still self-serving.

Back then, I frequently used the iconoclast formula to do the wrong thing—like cheating on my first wife, Angelique. Angelique and I were married in December of 1996, right after I graduated from college and started a job working as a CPA in Grand Rapids, Michigan. We had dated for a few years in college, and we were both very young when we got married. I had just turned twenty-two, and Angelique was still twenty. She was not even of legal age to drink alcohol at our wedding.

Angelique came from a very troubled home and pressed me hard to get married as a means to escape her dysfunctional family life. Marrying Angelique just seemed like the right thing to do—sort of. I had never had a relationship that lasted as long as ours had, a total of two years. I figured getting married was just what you did if you were still dating after college. As I mentioned, I was being a drone and following that prescribed path. But there was more in it for me: with her bad family situation, I felt like a knight in shining armor rescuing a damsel in distress. It felt good to marry her, and I thought she would be eternally grateful that I had rescued her from her home life.

After a few years, the honeymoon period had worn off, and we were faced with the real problems of marriage, ones that would require serious effort and work as a couple. But neither of us had the faith, knowledge, or interest to better the relationship. As a result, it became very toxic, legalistic, and transaction oriented. Everything we did for each other was negotiated. It was very much an arrangement of "You do this for me, and I will do this for you." Real love, backed with a pledge to uphold certain values, was completely absent from the relationship.

Time passed, and I found myself having affairs with other women. Several of them started as emotional connections at first but then became physical. To make the affairs work logistically, I used creativity to produce lies about my whereabouts. I used engineering to structure my time and maintain the appearances necessary to lie to both Angelique and the women with whom I was having affairs. In short, I was living a double life and using the iconoclast principles to successfully achieve it.

More than anything, I was a coward. I wanted to leave the marriage, but I was just too scared of the outcome. I worried that I would never see my daughters, that I would be ruined financially, and that my life from that point on would be difficult. Adultery seemed like a good solution to it all.

In 2005, Angelique found out what was going on. Unfortunately, at that point I had no confidence I could stay faithful to her. Despite trying to mend the relationship, the bottom line was I didn't love her anymore, and neither our relationship nor I was anchored to Christ. In 2007, our divorce was finally approved by the court.

Despite our problems, being unfaithful in marriage is the biggest mistake I have ever made in life, and I am sorry for it. I have asked for forgiveness from Christ and from Angelique, and I work every day to rectify it.

My second wife, Caroline, was married to a man who cheated on her. Not wanting to fail again in marriage, Caroline and I have committed our marriage to Christ and work hard to make it a loving, caring, and rewarding relationship for both of us. We have also tried to help other couples through the brokenness we have experienced by leading a marriage ministry at our church.

While adultery may have been the biggest mistake I made, it wasn't the only one. In early 2016, I finally admitted I had an addiction to pornography. This addiction started even before I was a teenager—around age twelve. It continued through both my marriages. It wasn't until I was forty-two years old that I decided it was time to get rid of the addiction.

As my faith grew stronger in Christ, I wanted to level up in my beliefs and actions. Consuming pornography was getting in the way leveling up in my faith. I could not claim to be doing God's will out in the open and fostering this habitual sin behind closed doors. My hypocrisy was just eating away at me, and I was losing confidence in myself.

Pornography has a dark reality. It is based on lies and creates addiction for many young men, such as the one I experienced, and serves as a roadblock to healthy sexual relationships with women. My pornography addiction began getting in the way of having a successful marriage with Caroline. When problems arose between us, as they are virtually guaranteed to do in relationships, it was too easy for me to meet my sexual needs through pornography rather than take the time to face our issues and work through our problems so that we could connect sexually through a healthy and caring marriage.

This time, though, rather than using the iconoclast formula for evil, I used it to do better—to level off my addiction to pornography.

The first question I asked was, Why are things the way they are? Well, upon further research and talking to some professionals in the field, I learned that looking at pornographic images over a long period of time chemically rewires your brain to become addicted to the material. Viewing pornographic images creates a chemical response in your brain, triggering a dopamine release. As a result, you feel good. And then you feel like you can't live without the sensation it provides. This is often why addictions like this one get worse and worse with time, as the addicted person seeks more and more material to maintain a high.

I soon realized that it didn't need to be this way. If I could get off the material, and stop reinforcing that chemical response, the addiction would slowly and progressively fade away. I then engineered a plan to remove pornographic material from my life. I slowly decreased the amount of pornography I consumed over a period of eight weeks. I began working with a therapist, who served as an accountability partner. And most importantly, I asked God for help. With the power of Christ, daily prayer, and a commitment to act on the plan I had implemented, I was cured from this addiction in July of 2016.

I haven't viewed pornography since, despite countless opportunities to reengage with the material on business trips alone and weekends when Caroline is on retreats with her girlfriends. But I don't have any desire to go back to the life I had. With God's assistance, I have been truly cured from this addiction. I'm so grateful for God's help and the iconoclast formula in curing this addiction, and I openly share my broken experience with other men as a means of helping my fellow brothers struggling with this addiction.

# Part 5 Summary and Questions

## CHAPTER SUMMARY

- My experience in gymnastics served as the foundation of my iconoclast thinking, combining creativity, engineering, and discipline.

- By challenging the way customers were shopping for new software as a business owner, I formed a habit of challenging thinking—others' and my own—further enforcing my iconoclast perspective.

- Iconoclasm can be used for good or bad, and I've applied the formula in both ways in my life.

## QUESTIONS TO CONSIDER

- What types of activities in your life have driven you to think creatively?

- When was the last time you questioned an existing way of doing things?

- When you think of a process or way of doing things that seems broken in your professional life, what comes to mind?

- When you think of a process or way of doing things that seems broken in your personal life, what comes to mind?

- How can you use the iconoclast formula to begin to make change?

# PART 6

# THE PANDEMIC EFFECT ON RELATIONSHIPS—AND ICONOCLAST SOLUTIONS

With a clear understanding of how iconoclasm can apply to your life, whether personal or professional, let's talk about how it applies to larger systems and societal problems that may arise—namely, the coronavirus pandemic.

While it was clear that the coronavirus created a panic that resulted in a complete shutdown of the US economy, it is not clear whether it was the right decision to do so and for what period of time. Whether you believe the government overstepped its authority in stopping the economy or not, the fact is that it did.

Further, this change has ushered in a series of new dynamics in our society—many of which will persist long after the pandemic ends. As I have discussed throughout this book, a change in underlying dynamics allows for us to challenge the existing paradigm and find new opportunities. So let's explore what the virus-driven shift in some of our societal dynamics looks like, as well as the opportunities it presents.

The new dynamics introduced by social distancing are far-reaching. Consider your work dynamic, for instance. For businesses, virtual meetings have become a perfectly acceptable means of working together professionally in a very short period of time. However, there is a difference between personal and professional relationships. While virtual meetings work extremely well for professional relationships, they don't necessarily suffice when it comes to personal relationships. Let's take a closer look at the difference between the two and the corresponding technologies that may or may not prove useful to facilitate each.

## Professional Relationships

Let's start with professional relationships. Just to give you a little context of where I'm coming from, I'll share a few details about my company. By now you know that Accounting Seed sells an accounting system. We primarily serve midmarket and small businesses with cloud-based technology. Our average sale is about $9,000 in licensing per year. As such, it has never made economic sense for my sales team to travel on-site to a prospect's location to close deals.

Technology has allowed us to do everything virtually, centralize our sales force, and provide more value to our customers through lower pricing.

Prior to starting my own business, I worked as a reseller in the Microsoft space, where I thought of my company as a regional firm serving the Baltimore and Washington, DC, area. It was a different business model, and providing a personal touch counted most, as the firm focused primarily on midmarket and enterprise customers. Plus, the average sale was much higher. Even back in the mid-2000s, sales for a product like this typically fell in the $50,000-to-$100,000 range. With the higher dollar volume came the need for more face-to-face meetings.

Meanwhile, Accounting Seed was born in the cloud. I was teleconferencing with people from the get-go. Out of the one thousand customers that have purchased the product to date, I have visited only just one or two in person. Only about half a dozen or so have come to my office in Columbia, Maryland. As such, working virtually isn't new for me or my team—it's what my company has been doing for the past ten years. Moreover, it has become the norm, serving as common practice for sales teams focused on the SMB market—at least in terms of cloud computing.

Many of my business relationships with customers and vendors over the past decade have been completely virtual, and the majority of them have been healthy, spurring repeat business despite the fact that we'd never met in person. I've used voice-over and digital media services from companies in California and contract services for development from companies in India and Russia, and I've worked with consultants all over the East Coast and in the Midwest as well. The internet has made finding collaborators, colleagues, and clients super simple. The trick to working with folks online is just starting out with smaller engagements where trust can be developed more quickly. Then, once trust is established, you can move onto larger engagements.

While cloud-based businesses have long embraced virtual work, other types of companies haven't always been amenable to this type of professional relationship. What the coronavirus has done is made the virtual approach completely mainstream in the professional world. Further, it has established a paradigm going forward. Now that we've gotten used to working virtually, in the post-pandemic environment it will seem crazy to travel on-site to work with someone when it's not totally necessary. But it will require us to shift our thinking.

## EMBRACING A VIRTUAL FIRST MINDSET

I truly believe that as a result of the coronavirus pandemic, professional relationships will embrace a virtual-first mindset. There is no requirement for a personal connection in most professional relationships. As a result, having a virtual one is just fine. You could even argue that a lot of people don't want to mix personal and corporate connections and that a virtual relationship reinforces a level of formality that is appropriate for a corporate relationship. It is simply easier to be less personal when we're dealing with a relationship virtually.

Also, just think of the time workers save in eliminating non-value-added travel, from hours spent on back-to-back traffic on highways, crowded and backlogged security lines at airports, and searching for impossible-to-find parking spots in congested urban sprawl.

With a new perspective, we can better coordinate business trips for less time spent on the road and more savings overall if and when travel is absolutely necessary. For instance, travel to see business partners can often be combined with attending trade shows and events that they plan to attend as well.

The timeline for an engagement or relationship may also dictate whether travel is necessary. For example, if you're planning to work with a contractor or business associate for less than twelve months, you probably won't even consider planning a trip to see them. A two-year engagement may merit a visit as part of other business travel plans, allowing for face-to-face connection without too much additional effort. If you're planning a long-term relationship, a formal visit up front to establish the relationship is most likely a worthwhile choice, but additional trips may not be necessary once things are moving.

When determining whether a particular situation would benefit from an in-person visit, we can consider some of the downsides I've mentioned, as well as the benefits. Physical connection provides us with the ability to better understand a person and their perspective. Having had a physical interaction with a person also helps us gauge their intensity. In meeting someone physically, we can gain a better understanding of how important certain items are to them, as well as the points they emphasize most. It is like trying to read a book with a pair of reading glasses on when you haven't ever used them before—it provides a bit of additional clarity.

> Physical connection provides us with the ability to better understand a person and their perspective.

An effective working relationship doesn't require us to be in the constant presence of another person physically once we have met them. The virtual setting allows for us to see them and be reminded of their nature. With an in-person interaction to reflect on, our minds will fill in the blanks.

Seeing someone—even via video—also goes a long way. I have worked with contractors with whom I speak only via telephone. I must say I find this very inferior to actual virtual conferencing. Audio only leaves a lot of communication out in terms of facial expressions and body language. Seeing someone as well as hearing them allows you to read their body language and answer the following questions:

- What is important to them?

- What needs to be clarified?

- What could you—or they—possibly be misunderstanding?

If you're refusing to engage in video calls, you're really putting yourself—and your business relationships—at a disadvantage. It's old-school thinking, and customers and clients are bound to notice. You must reevaluate the way you communicate in a professional setting.

## A Shift in the Way We Communicate

With every new type of technology that we adopt, it seems a new level of unofficial rules are introduced in terms of when and how to use that technology in relation to the other platforms out there. Further, it seems to me like the formality hierarchy of professional communication has been building over the past several years but has been fully realized during the virus panic.

Have you noticed in the last couple of years that nobody ever picks up their phone anymore unless they know exactly who is calling? If they don't recognize the number, they let it go to voice mail, assuming that if it is important enough, they can just call back—or vice versa. This phenomenon has actually become a huge problem in polling and political elections. Professional polling companies have not been able to engage the public by phone to ask them what their thoughts are with regards to political candidates. This has created misinformation and inaccuracy in political polls. They just aren't pre-dictive of what will happen in an actual election anymore.

Why this shift? With the introduction of texting and direct

messaging on social apps, phone calls have become a very formal means of communication. Most people are more comfortable with a first-level contact via text rather than a phone call. Getting on the phone is reserved for serious business. I would argue that the formality of communication in the business community has an established hierarchy, as shown below:

1. Direct message on social media
2. Email
3. Phone call
4. Virtual meeting
5. Texting
6. Physical meeting

## DIRECT MESSAGE ON SOCIAL MEDIA

Let's start with LinkedIn and direct messaging on social media. With no one answering their phones anymore and the uncertainty surrounding the validity of email addresses, the new sales cold call is a direct message and friend request on LinkedIn. I can't tell you how many times a day I get requests and messages on LinkedIn from those trying to sell me their services. This is just plain old-school soliciting on a newer platform. The person is essentially knocking on office doors but online. The reality is this is a significant improvement for both the solicitor and solicitee, as they don't take much effort to send and they're also very easy to ignore.

## EMAIL

If I do happen to be interested in connecting with someone on LinkedIn, I will ask for their email address as the next level up. Email is still the primary means of external communications; however, this is really not the case for internal interactions anymore. Products like Slack have really taken over as internal communication systems, replacing email at a lot of forward-thinking companies. Since I'm in sales and business management, I still have to communicate with people outside my company—that's the primary reason I still pay attention to my email. But I use Slack to communicate inside the company because it combines the convenience of direct messaging and emailing all in one interface and allows for a user to see the thread of conversation between a common group of people much more easily. Products like Chatter in Salesforce also give a contextualized conversation around a data record. Slack and Salesforce simply provide efficient communications around subject matters internally that are lost with an external email system. The bottom line is these tools make digital collaboration easier and faster.

## PHONE CALL / VIRTUAL CALL

After emails have been exchanged, it's logical to progress to a phone call or virtual call. A virtual call is the preferred method of communication for most business people, but not everyone wants to be seen all the time. Most of the time people send out conferencing credentials that allow for images to be displayed; however, not until the pandemic did I see people regularly showing themselves on camera. With most of us working from home in relative isolation, people crave the opportunity to see others. As a result, they're treating others as they would like to be treated by turning on their own cameras.

Often, people choose to dial into virtual meetings from their cell phones when they can't log in from a computer. Though I do this myself and see other leaders doing it when they're in the car or on a train, it's really a less desirable conferencing mechanism.

whether an employee is working hard or not, and the pandemic has forced us to think about employee productivity. When I came to think about it, I asked myself: "Why didn't I treat the employees who I've hired to work in the office this same way?" Working remotely, I can't see anybody. I don't know what they're doing hour to hour, so I have to manage them based on metrics as well as through those daily check-ins. The way I worked with remote employees has become the company standard—and it will be going forward.

For every employee we hire, I'm going to imagine them working remotely 100 percent of the time, even when they will be working in the office. If I can set up an effective routine to manage them remotely, then I will always be able to manage them well in the office.

As a growing company, the biggest challenges we've had in hiring people is determining who is going to train them, manage them, and measure their success. This is a common issue for companies that are expanding at a very fast pace. When you don't have the logistics nailed down, you can easily waste a ton of money on mistakes. I'm always intrigued by companies that increase their head count from just a handful of employees to several hundred all at once. You better believe these companies are wasting a lot of money, as the blind are most definitely leading the blind. In most businesses, there's only so much you can grow at once while still delivering a quality offering.

The other thing we will be asking during hiring going forward is "What is your work-at-home situation?" Of course, it is illegal to ask about marriage and children in a job interview, but it is always reassuring when a prospective hire offers up this information, as it demonstrates their transparency. The reality is most people can have a successful work-from-home situation, even with children, spouses, or parents around. However, it does require the right setup and equipment. An employee who expects to be productive working at the dining room table with four kids at home is probably operating under very unrealistic expectations. However, if they have a private office away from the kids' playroom, there's no reason they can't be a successful work-from-home employee.

We also will ask about their discipline. The way they plan to keep themselves disciplined and motivated when working from home will be a key determinant in whether or not they get the job.

## EMPLOYER AND EMPLOYEE RELATIONSHIPS

The coronavirus pandemic has completely shifted how we will hire knowledge workers in the future. A knowledge worker is really just defined as anyone who works at a computer for their job. Nowadays, I would say unless you have a position in labor or management in manufacturing, construction, distribution, travel, hospitality, or the personal services industries, you probably qualify as a knowledge worker.

Over the past five years, my staff has grown from about seven people to fifty people. With the growth of my team, the requests to work from home at least part time have just gone up and up and up. Prior to the pandemic, my stance on letting people work from home was to make decisions on a case-by-case basis rather than instituting a blanket company policy. Having a trusted relationship with the employee was the key parameter for letting them work from home or not. I defined a trusted relationship as the following:

1.  Employee had worked at our company for over one year.

2.  They had been through a review cycle and received positive feedback.

3.  They had managed their own chart of work effectively and proved that they would ask for more work when they were

not busy.

When we started two new employees during the shutdown, all these rules went out the window. Everyone was working from home, and as a result, we had to establish a new definition of trust. It became the following:

1. They responded to inquiries quickly.

2. They were insightful and asked intelligent questions.

3. They learned from their interactions and built on their existing knowledge.

4. They set their own goals for getting things done.

5. They frequently volunteered to do more.

Being forced to work remotely has highlighted the fact that we have a false trust in physically observing someone working at their desk. It is what is going on in their brain that matters, and seeing them physically doesn't do much when it comes to assessing that. In fact, just like a blind person relies more heavily on other senses to figure out what is going on, working virtually has arguably forced us to hone our assessment skills and operate with a heightened observation of how employees interact with each and with customers.

> Being forced to work remotely has highlighted the fact that we have a false trust in physically observing someone working at their desk.

## THE VIRTUAL MANAGER

We must also think more deeply about management with a remote workforce. How we get along with others becomes less of an issue in a virtual environment, as there's less watercooler and cross talk between employees—but what becomes even more important is the relationship between an employee and their manager. When you're working virtually, management becomes a crucial skill set, as the manager needs to read between the lines and understand what's going on without the privilege of being able to drop by a subordinate's office.

The virtual manager will need to have a firm understanding of the level of effort necessary to perform the tasks assigned to the employee. An ongoing review and audit of work will be critical.

## CHANGING OFFICE STRATEGIES

Our office strategy has also changed. We hired our first employee in Europe in the summer of 2019. For the nine months prior to the virus outbreak, I had built a plan to open up an office near London and in Sydney, Australia. The virus completely changed my mind when it came to my strategy. I realized that all my workers in foreign territories could be remote. They just needed access to an office facility like Regus. Regus is a supplier of coworking spaces where employees can have face-to-face meetings on some kind of consistent basis, such as weekly or monthly. Most people are attracted to this type of flexibility, which creates an incentive for them to work at your company while keeping overhead low.

As we consider the shifts in professional and personal relationships, it's important to realize that those spending all day working remotely will have little to no tolerance for attending social events virtually. Humans crave connection, and remote employees will want to have in-person interactions to counter their virtual professional existence. In fact, having those experiences will be key to their success and happiness in life.

Another thing to note: I have worked from home in three separate jobs, and what I can say about it is there is an eighteen-month love affair that eventually wears off. The infatuation period ends eventually, and employees start to crave office interaction at least two to three days per week.

With remote workers that are 100 percent out of the office due to geography, the company would be well served to invest in their travel quarterly so they get out to the office and build some in-person relationships too. While scaling back on office space is a new legitimate strategy, it also requires an investment in some physical presence in the form of a part-time office arrangement or travel for events to keep employees sane and satisfied. Overall, though, virtual communication will provide an effective structure for most businesses.

Meanwhile, personal relationships are a different story.

## Personal Relationships

While the virus-driven shutdown has revealed that virtual platforms provide a great solution for professional relationships, that's not the case when it comes to personal relationships. The restrictions have shown that virtual connections are an awful substitute for in-person interactions. The shutdown provided proof we are safe from the virtual future portrayed in many science fiction films like *Surrogates* and *Ready Player One*. Physical connection is just too important.

Of course, we have different kinds of personal relationships that operate on a number of different levels. When you think about how many deep personal relationships you have, it's likely a relatively small amount given the limitations of your time and emotional energy. The close relationships in my life come from my professional group at YPO, my church small group, some of my neighbors, my family, and my closest friends. When I do the math, it adds up to about sixty people total. Perhaps if I really pushed myself and didn't work as many hours as I do, the number could be higher—maybe two hundred people—but that seems like a pretty big stretch. I know plenty of people who have far fewer than sixty close relationships in their lives. Regardless of how many people are part of your inner circle, with regards to deep personal relationships, virtual interaction just doesn't work that well—especially when it comes to giving someone a hug.

Next up are those acquaintance relationships, those with whom you work, worship, or collaborate professionally. Perhaps you'd like to have a closer relationship with them, but you settle for the fact that neither of you really has time to spend together outside the occasional party or social gathering. A virtual solution won't really work for this group of people in your life either. If you couldn't make time for them in person—you're probably not going to make the effort to do so online. Still, virtual technology is better than nothing. As such, it has and will continue to be used the same way the telephone has been used over the past one hundred years—as a second-tier means of connection. With that said, it does have its place, especially in these times.

## VIRTUAL SOCIAL GATHERINGS

With that in mind, soon after the shutdown began, I was shocked to see how many invitations to virtual happy hours, parties, and lunches began pouring in from various groups to which I belong. These events weren't already on the books. For example, while my church small group meets every other Saturday night and my YPO group connects on a monthly basis, none of these gatherings had been regular occurrences prior to the pandemic.

What became really interesting during the shutdown was the format of those new gatherings. For example one of the neighbors in our subdevelopment threw a family dance party on Facebook Live and served as the DJ. We put the Facebook page up on our living room television, and the kids shot videos of themselves dancing. The event provided somewhat of a real shared experience and was kind of entertaining. However, I think the amusement truly came from our efforts to connect in a creative way rather than the event being something fun that we would want to repeat.

While virtual socialization is certainly not a replacement for in-person interaction, I do believe there is a market for it—particularly when it comes to the under-eighteen demographic. Last year, after my son, who loved video games, passed away, I bought a Sony PlayStation VR set. I wanted to feel closer to him, and I thought the set would impress him. The virtual reality headset is a game changer, as it makes the experience feel real. Why wouldn't teenagers want to meet people in a kind of a chat room, especially now that the stigma of that being awkward or weird has gone away? Teenagers and kids without cars will certainly use something like that, even when the experience is accompanied by regular in-person interaction at school and beyond. And parents will love it, as it is physically safe.

With the restrictions on in-person interaction, internet dating sites like Match.com are also implementing services for virtual connection as a first step in internet or blind dating—a service that will likely stick around long term. How great would it be to be able to go on a virtual first date with someone as a next step over a traditional phone call? I used Match.com prior to settling down with my current wife, and I can tell you I would have appreciated something like FaceTime or a virtual headset prior to meeting in person. Rather than meeting someone at a Starbucks for fifteen minutes in order to leave yourself the ability to bail if the interaction is too awkward, you can stay very safe using FaceTime or some kind of virtual environment as a next step. The virus has just opened the door for all this being okay.

## IMPLEMENTING STRUCTURE IN VIRTUAL GATHERINGS

With the idea that virtual platforms aren't going anywhere when it comes to personal relationships, let's talk about what works structurally. Out of the various gatherings and parties that I attended virtually during the pandemic, I found the ones that worked best were with groups that already met on a regular schedule and had an established pattern of in-person interaction.

For example, out of all the groups that I attended online, my church small group probably translated best. In the church small group, which comprised a number of married couples, we had a methodology of meeting that was pretty well defined prior to the shutdown. We would have a topic of focus, which we would all read about prior to the session, and then we would go around the room sharing our thoughts on it—typically limiting the amount of time each of us spoke (about five minutes per person and eight minutes per couple). The person who was speaking always chose the next person to go when they finished sharing what they had to say. These parameters made for a very efficient virtual meeting. Although it felt less personal to hold the meeting online, the experience wasn't frustrating or disappointing in the new format.

The problem with attending a happy hour or another event without a preestablished structure is that it is just a mess of people on the phone. There has to be some kind of intentionality around taking turns or sharing that just isn't necessary if you're navigating a physical space together. In an in-person setting, you just wander from conversation to conversation and person to person. If you're bored, you simply move on to another group of people talking. And nobody questions whether you're paying attention or thinking about something else at a real-life party, the way they do in a large-group virtual setting. As such, even social gatherings need structure in a virtual setting.

Eventually, technology will advance to mimic the kinds of individual conversations one can have at a cocktail party—we're just not quite there yet. And until then, we need to do something about this shortcoming.

In several meetings during the pandemic, I got to experience virtual rooms in Zoom, in which the moderator institutes breakout sessions via smaller rooms to which participants can retreat before joining the larger conversation. Breakout rooms are an excellent addition to the technology, but the rooms have to be defined by the moderator, who must place participants in each one. Meanwhile, in a happy hour, those "breakout sessions" happen naturally—you wander from subgroup to subgroup on your own. We need a way to replicate that. I believe the gaming industry will figure this out way before the teleconferencing industry does. It seems like a much bigger leap for GoToMeeting, Zoom, and Webex than it would be for a Sony PlayStation, Nintendo, or Microsoft gaming system.

The pandemic has delivered for us one major benefit to virtual interactions that I should mention: the elimination of feeling socially awkward while having them. I was amazed to find that FaceTime came out in 2010. As of this writing, the product has been on the market for ten years, and yet it seemed kind of weird to use it prior to this outbreak. Now I have friends and family arranging for FaceTime calls on the weekends; it's just become a way of life. The same is true of Zoom; widely available teleconferencing software has been around for nine years.

However, the social awkwardness it prompted drove many to make traditional phone calls rather than using a video interface. Obviously, that's not the case anymore. This is a powerful change in dynamics that is going to lead to all kinds of opportunities in the post-pandemic economy.

## Other Pandemic-Induced Relationship Shifts

Coronavirus has also changed the way we purchase products and services and interact with their vendors. Prior to the pandemic, I purchased a new car. I traded my gas-guzzling Chevy Camaro for a fully electric Chevy Bolt. Why did I make the switch? I purchased the Bolt to help the environment by consuming fewer fossil fuels. The best thing we can do for the planet is leave the oil in the ground as much as possible, as far as I am concerned.

I absolutely love the Bolt, by the way, and recommend everyone who can purchase one does. Not only is it a quiet and peaceful driving machine, I just can't get over how cool it is to have my house essentially become my gas station. With that in mind, I decided to get a level-two charging station installed in my house. The level-one charger will charge the vehicle at about four miles per hour, while a level two does the same work about four times as fast, charging it at about fifteen miles per hour. Between the level-two charger and the 250-mile range on the vehicle, I can drive all over the Baltimore-Washington, DC, corridor without any anxiety or need to plan my week with regards to charging.

Let's backtrack a little. Buying the charger meant I needed to have it installed. Like many people, I don't remember which home technicians I have worked with in the past, so I typically use the site

Home Advisor to find a new technician when I need one. This was no exception. I found an electrician who could do the work: James, an independent gentleman who works out of Frederick, Maryland, about forty-five minutes from my house.

James wanted to find out more about the house, and Home Advisor software scheduled an on-site visit for him to come check out the job in person and give me an estimate. James quickly sent me a text asking me if I could do a FaceTime call in lieu of the physical site visit for the estimate. Being a lover of technology and wanting to wipe something else off my schedule, I said sure. I was happy to give it a try. I was pretty amazed with how the experience turned out. James had me FaceTime and walk around the house. He had me first walk out to the garage, where I directed my screen to the place I wanted the charger installed.

We then discussed the options while I continued walking around the garage, flipping the phone's camera between my face and my surroundings so he could get an idea of the beam structure—all via FaceTime. We then walked down into the basement, where he instructed me to find the fuse box. As an experienced electrician, James knew the important questions to ask in order to determine what he would need to complete the electrical work I was requesting. He then proceeded to give me an estimate later that day. With that simple, quick interaction, we scheduled the work.

Another example that comes to mind occurred during the pandemic as well. I wanted to keep shooting videos for my website. My full-time videographer lives north of Baltimore, about a forty-five minute drive from the office. I didn't want to have him come on-site just to help me set up some lights for the temporary studio I was creating at my desk. So I used what I learned from James and had a FaceTime call with him.

I flipped my camera around so he could see my point of view as I walked to our marketing closet, where all his equipment is stored, and showed him everything on the shelves. With his guidance, I grabbed the right lights and set them up properly.

In the post-coronavirus era, this will become the new normal. Our current circumstances have mainstreamed the notion of using virtual tools intelligently to save time and energy. And the iconoclast formula can help you make the most of these shifts, questioning why things are the way they are and crafting solutions to take advantage of them.

# Part 6 Summary and Questions

## CHAPTER SUMMARY

- The coronavirus shutdown has had different effects on professional and personal relationships. It has proved virtualization was very suitable for professional relationships but a poor substitute for in-person interaction in relationships.

- Communication in the virtual age has fostered the adoption of new social norms with the uses of different technologies for communication.

- Many companies will adopt a policy of hiring remote workers for the right experience over hiring locals.

- Employers in the knowledge worker space will be forced to accommodate employees working from home to retain their talent.

- Management of employees in the post-pandemic era will require a different approach, as we don't have the luxury of simply stopping by their offices.

## QUESTIONS TO CONSIDER

- Would you rather hire a knowledge worker who is local but does not have the exact experience you are looking for or hire a remote worker with the perfect credentials?

- What will be the hardest part about managing knowledge workers remotely at your organization?

- How often do you think a team of knowledge workers needs

to meet in person to form meaningful relationships?

- How can you employ the iconoclast formula to address some of the paradigm shifts the pandemic has introduced?

# PART 7

# THE PANDEMIC EFFECT ON CONSUMER PURCHASING

I believe I bought my first book on Amazon.com somewhere around 1996—the year I graduated college. I was living in Grand Rapids, Michigan, at the time, and I distinctly remember how crazy it felt to buy a book online when I was so used to going to Barnes & Noble or Borders. At those stores, I had the opportunity to inspect the product and leave with no doubt in my mind that I had gotten what I paid for. After buying online for the first time, I was left wondering if the book would ever come. I wondered whether it would be in good condition, what would happen if I wanted to return it, and whether or not I had just been scammed.

From that year forward, I probably approached online retailing like most Americans did. I took it slow, making sure I didn't find myself in the midst of a scheme to steal my credit card number.

But about a decade ago, I started to get really frustrated with brick-and-mortar retailers altogether, especially when it came to holidays and birthdays. It didn't make any sense to me that when I wanted to send something to a friend or family member in another city or state, I'd have to go to the store to buy the gift and then make my way to a shipping provider like Parcel Plus or the UPS Store and have them package it and ship it for an additional fee—all while adding more time to the process. At least twice, I purchased my mom a Macy's gift card at a physical store and mailed it to her, only to find out that it had been stolen and I had no recourse for getting my money back. In 2010, the deal was sealed—I began exclusively buying Christmas gifts online for family and friends with whom I wouldn't be spending the holidays. I just didn't want to have to deal with shipping, so it was an absolute no-brainer.

From there, online shopping became a gradually growing trend for me, which has been similar to the purchasing style of the nation. From 2011 on, every year at Christmas I would not only purchase gifts for friends and relatives that I wouldn't see during the holidays, but I also began purchasing them for friends and family with whom I would be spending time. I would buy just a few more things online than I would at retail stores each year. It was a lot of work to deal with the mall and traffic, and in my mind, I had more important things to do with my time.

As I purchased more gifts for others online, I started shopping virtually for items I needed personally as well. I also noticed the variety and availability of products in retail stores diminishing, making it impossible to find many of the things I needed—and ratcheting up the appeal of online shopping even more. Even with large brick-and-mortar retailers like Home Depot or Target, you spend a lot of time hunting for the product and asking store employees where things are. Meanwhile, Amazon makes finding what you need so damn easy, all while storing all of your credit card and shipping information—making that purchase truly one click away. It's no wonder that it is fast becoming a monopoly.

But the reality is we don't value a unique buying experience nearly as much as we think we do, especially when it comes to shopping online. The core factors we are looking for in making a purchasing decision are product reviews, a good price, and the comfort in knowing that if something goes wrong, the company will work with us to make it right. Amazon does all these things so well that there's no real incentive to go anywhere else. And as the world has grappled with the effects of the pandemic, online shopping has experienced even more of a surge in popularity. In August of 2020, for example, Adobe Analytics reported that US online sales had increased 55 percent year over year.[7]

These days, when I do buy at a brick-and-mortar store, I do it because they provide a niche service, offering the kind of convenience I have come to expect, as well as multiple items related to the activity or purpose for which I am shopping. For example, during the shutdown of the economy, I wanted to buy more CrossFit gear for my house. Although it's possible to buy these things on Amazon, it's way more practical to buy them from a manufacturer like Rogue or Concept2, companies that actually make the equipment and can bundle your items with the other things you may be interested in using while working out. It is much easier than having to weed through thousands of product pages on Amazon to find what you need.

---

7    "Adobe Digital Economy Index," Adobe Analytics, August 2020, https://www.adobe.com/content/dam/www/us/en/experience-cloud/digital-insights/pdfs/adobe_analytics-digital-economy-index-2020.pdf.

# The Steady Struggle of Traditional Retail

Meanwhile, even without the recent adverse world events, traditional retail has been in dire straits for many years. It has undergone a consistent, steady decline as online retail continues to skyrocket. I remember first hearing the term *retail apocalypse* in 2019, when businessinsider.com and usatoday.com reported that nine thousand US retail locations had closed that year alone. That represented an increase of 59 percent from the prior year's closings, which also reached record high numbers—with the previous all-time high occurring in 2012. Even newer retailers like Forever 21 and H&M that have been capitalizing on the fast-fashion movement were starting to experience financial trouble and close locations as they faced competition from businesses operating entirely online.

With three teen daughters who want to go to the mall all the time, I've seen this decline happen firsthand as we watched shops close left and right recently. This being said, our local mall has struggled immensely for the past fifteen years, at least. It has only been able to weather the storm by transitioning many of the retail stores to restaurants and service providers. For example, the Sears is now an arcade, and the automotive shop is now an Uncle Julio's.

The retail apocalypse is a vicious cycle. The less brick-and-mortar retailers there are, the more people shop online—and the more people shop online, the more the traditional retailers struggle. I finally gave up going to the hardware store for traditional home-repair items. I just buy them on Amazon, along with many of the products I use every day. With a simple search, I can find everything from furnace filters and screwdrivers to light-switch covers and light bulbs and have them delivered to my house the next day. It's a vast improvement over hunting them down in a store and trying to find a disgruntled part-time employee when I can't locate them myself—someone who is already talking to six people in front of me and who wouldn't have been that interested in helping me locate my product in the first place.

## THE CRYSTALLIZATION OF E-COMMERCE

The pandemic has only accelerated the death of retail as we know it, as people make fewer discretionary purchases in general and avoid leaving their homes when they do decide to shop. What brick-and-mortar operations will survive when things reopen? Experiences—food, entertainment, and niche experience shopping.

I don't think I need to say much about food and entertainment, since those are pretty self-explanatory. During the shutdown, many of us found ourselves desperate to visit a movie theater or dine in a restaurant with friends. When those locations reopened, we were there. Niche experience shopping refers to a shopping experience in which value is added—in the form of guidance and expertise, for instance.

The best example of niche experience shopping I've seen is my local running store. I've run two full marathons and eight half marathons in my lifetime, and I typically run 5Ks three times a week in the summer. As such, good running shoes are important to me. What I love most about going to the running store is that they fit me with custom insoles right then and there. They also continue to measure the supination and pronation—fancy terms for the angle at which your foot strikes the ground, and that can be corrected with the right shoes—in my stride as I run on a treadmill with the help of cameras. This kind of enriched physical retail experience is what is going to make it in the new economy. With that in mind, we have to talk about the new dynamic that the pandemic has ushered in and what it will entail.

## THE NEW UNDERLYING DYNAMIC

The fact that the world has formed a habit of buying anything and everything online in a matter of twelve-plus weeks during the shutdown will have an irreversible impact on the traditional retail market. While we have long shopped online for certain items, we have crystallized a new pattern of looking for everything and anything we may want online first, before even considering stepping foot in a store. And the efficiency and convenience online shopping provide means that, for many of us, it's just not worth reverting to the old way of doing things.

In late September of 2020, after seven months of minimizing our journeys out of the home, my daughter and I agreed that it seemed weird to go into a retail store to find what we wanted after living an online-first existence for so long. With that in mind, I'm sure the Targets and the Walmarts of the world will still be around alongside those cool niche retail experiences, but most other brick-and-mortar retail businesses are going to find themselves struggling to keep their doors open.

> **The fact that the world has formed a habit of buying anything and everything online in a matter of twelve-plus weeks during the shutdown will have an irreversible impact on the traditional retail market.**

## THE FUTURE OF THE SHOPPING MALL

In 2016, I offered to take my daughter and her friends to a nearby mall.

"No thanks, Dad—that's a zombie mall," she replied. It was a phrase I'd never heard before, but when I started to notice just how many retail stores were closing, it started to make sense. I began to see YouTube videos popping up in my stream that featured tours of abandoned malls or highlighted their closing. Several of the videos even captured mall funerals of sorts, in recognition of the emotional impact of the end of an era.

What I noticed more than anything is that the concept of shopping malls needs an iconoclastic approach. They need to be reengineered.

One day, I was shopping at the Columbia Mall after having dinner at P. F. Chang's with my daughters. Inside the mall, it seemed like there was an exceptional amount of stores closed. It felt like at least one-third, maybe even half, of them were shut. It was odd and depressing to see and also brought into sharp relief a scary reality.

Malls have served as the modern downtown for many communities. As they shutter, jobs end, too, and more empty space means more risk. Right now, I live right outside Baltimore, which has been the murder capital of the world for the past several years. As a father, I fear dropping off three teenage girls in a place that has become a hotbed for crime and little else—without shops or things to do, the mall is a dangerous space. This has certainly been the case for Security Mall, the mall next to the Social Security Administration Building near I-70 and the Baltimore beltway. It had been a clean and well-maintained shopping haven in the 1950s and 1960s, but things have since gone downhill, especially over the past ten years. Even though the area is populated by many citizens who have well-paying jobs, with few stores or activities to keep people's attention, it's become unsafe.

Despite the challenges faced by so many malls around the

country—including our local operation—it dawned on me that there is a huge opportunity for shopping malls if they simply break away from their existing paradigm: providing a storefront to a traditional retailer that buys and distributes merchandise to consumers.

In the old days, that was the only way to sell, of course. Now that we have the internet—and with it the chance to purchase and ship any product we can imagine—that existing paradigm no longer holds up. As such, the mall model should change too. Consider this: What if the malls did some remodeling, redistributing and repricing the space they offered so that floors were broken down into little booths—much like those carts that populate hallways between the stores today? The malls could become product expos, where manufacturers could rent a small eight-by-ten space to showcase their products. With just one or two staffers sampling their items at a kiosk, presenting their inventory, and offering customers the ability to place an order that would arrive at their door in short order, the mall space could be used much more economically.

Meanwhile, with more products to check out and an experiential element, the expo would become an attraction of sorts. People could go out to dinner at popular mall-based chains like P. F. Chang's and the Cheesecake Factory and then walk around browsing products and learning about what's new. Also, they wouldn't be faced with the burden of lugging bags back to their car, since most products would be shipped directly to their home! In truth, the only way to save the future of retail is to rethink it by adopting these kinds of outside-the-box ideas and implementing them.

## THE RISE OF FLEX SPACE

The second thing you'll see when you begin to analyze retail is that a lot of nontraditional retail businesses are setting up shop in what would be considered "flex spaces." The flex space, by definition, can be used for many purposes—office space, manufacturing, distribution, or entertainment. In fact, my current office is located in a flex space—a single-story office park. In the same block of space is a karate dojo, gymnastics gym, CrossFit gym, laser-tag arena, a niche insurance agency, and a civil engineering firm. Prior to the decline of retail, many were using traditional retail spaces, but as those areas shuttered, they sought another option in the form of flex space—one that will only increase in popularity as malls continue to decline.

I've looked into building several businesses over my career. Around the year 2000, I considered establishing an age-group gymnastics franchise. I had built a plan around a business called Kartwheel Kids, a recreational gymnastics program for school-age children that would provide kids with the opportunity to learn some basic gymnastics but largely serve as an opportunity for them to engage in recreational athletics. The business model was built around after-school activities and summer camps.

When I was researching the business plan, I was shopping for a retail environment to rent. The more expensive retail environments were all measured based on the traffic right outside the site—meaning the number of cars that were driving by on the road outside the strip malls where these spaces were located. That was a problem. Why? Not only has the internet attacked retailers directly with convenience and efficiency, but the way it has changed our purchasing habits also means we are not out driving as much. Thus, we have fewer opportunities to notice traditional brick-and-mortar businesses in our communities. This is somewhat of a secondary or sideways attack on traditional retail. The reduced traffic has greatly affected other businesses' visibility. As such, businesses also have to break out of the existing paradigm when it comes to advertising and self-promotion.

Sapwood Cellars is a microbrewery that is also located in the flex space right outside our offices. They have really great beer, but you would never know they existed if you didn't have the internet or know someone who loved the place already. They are buried in the way, way back of the park. However, the flex space allows them to keep their overhead low and offer a great product at a great price. In addition, they have cultivated an excellent referral network. Combined with simple online advertising and some mailers, they have been able to thrive. Other microbreweries are following suit, adopting a similar model to promote their product successfully as the retail landscape continues to change.

As consumers, we can also consider our current habits and apply the iconoclast formula to make meaningful change.

# Applying the Iconoclast Formula as a Consumer

I have unequivocally applied the iconoclast formula to my diet and relationship to food. I really started dieting when I turned thirty-five. I had been through a divorce and just didn't have the time to work out the way I could in my twenties. I tried several programs, including Jenny Craig, the South Beach Diet, Atkins, and Weight Watchers. Regardless of the program, I found it extremely difficult to make the caloric cutoff prescribed for my weight-loss goal. I tried for years to fit all my protein, fat, and carb needs into three meals a day—eliminating snacks to make that calorie limit. Along the way, I'd have some success, only to backslide. Ultimately, without snacks, I couldn't make it through the day. In 2017, many years after I had begun my dieting journey, I finally decided to challenge the existing paradigm and ask, Why are we eating three meals a day? Where does this practice come from?

Well, the answer to this question is that nobody knows exactly when this became the standard societal practice. Many historians guess that it probably began in the late 1700s, with the onset of the agricultural revolution. In the late eighteenth century, the notion of three meals a day was adopted as the true standard. Farming had advanced significantly, and food was readily available all the time. Food began to be sold in bundles three times a day, due in part to the business proposition backing this consumption pattern. It allowed manufacturers and distributors of food to sell more of their product. It's similar to the corporate takeover of holidays like Christmas, in which retailers have capitalized on the holiday in hopes of selling more stuff. Without the commercial drive, the Christmas season would actually resemble Easter.

Following the iconoclast formula, the underlying dynamic that changed in the late 1700s was that food was available everywhere all the time. With more product, it was businesses' prerogative to sell people more of it. That dynamic remains today.

Further exacerbating the issue of abundance—especially in countries like America—is the fact that the food we eat now compared to the late 1700s is so highly processed. As a result, many of the food products on the market have little nutritional value and lots of empty calories. When combined with the dynamic promoted by the abundance of motorized vehicles and desk jobs—that we don't walk or get much exercise over the course of our day—we've seen waistlines expand over the years as well.

It wasn't until I discovered intermittent fasting that I even thought I could survive on fewer than three meals a day. It sounded absolutely crazy to me. As a kid, I thought I would die if I skipped eating for a day. But once I began researching, I realized that for the majority of humanity's existence, we have survived on much less than we do now. Think about it: people have been around for about two hundred thousand years, and we have only been eating three meals per day for just over two hundred of them—or .1 percent of our existence as a species! The rest of the time, we have been hunters and gatherers. There was no guarantee that we'd get a regular meal. If we couldn't catch something to eat, we simply went without.

## OMAD

In truth, our bodies have not evolved much over the past two hundred thousand years—though the world around us has. With that in mind, I started intermittent fasting right away. I started on what's called a five-two program, eating five days a week and taking two days off. Most people who have done this practice suggest you do not make the days consecutive; as such, I stopped eating on Mondays and Thursdays. It worked extremely well, and because I had to balance my caloric intake with my morning workouts at CrossFit, those workouts became more productive too.

I continued to experiment, trying several different fasting techniques. All worked well and had their place—I just had to find the one that was right for me. Eventually, I settled on the "one meal a day," or OMAD, plan. Now, seven days a week I just eat dinner. I try to eat at the same time every night, stopping when I feel full and avoiding snacking later in the evening. This approach has kept me fit and lean. If I've gained more weight than I'd like, I'll take a full fast day, skipping meals altogether to get back on track. OMAD is a great solution for me, but of course it's not for everyone.

How do you find what works for you? You have to start by challenging the paradigm. You have to ask, "Why are things the way they are?" When I determined that the underlying dynamic of eating three meals a day was based on a business and profit proposition, I decided to engineer a plan for change. I would increase the scarcity of food in my life by consuming just a single meal plan per day. After executing the plan, I've found that I'm better for it.

## THE RISE OF FOOD DELIVERY APPS

Although the virus did not change the way I eat—I still have just one meal a day—it certainly changed the way I shop for food. Being a busy entrepreneur prior to the shutdown, I typically ate out for almost every meal. On Tuesdays and weekend nights, I would have dinner with my family at a traditional sit-down restaurant; however, every other night of the week I would often choose a fast-casual meal in the interest of time.

When the pandemic hit, I, like so many other individuals and families, embraced online ordering and home delivery food services. It's amazing how many restaurants in the fast-casual space have an app for ordering. I was first introduced to this concept by Domino's Pizza, which has a fantastic app that makes ordering easy and convenient. There are about three other pizza places locally that have good food, but I found myself gravitating to Domino's just because it was so easy to order what I wanted and I didn't have to talk to anyone, much less read my credit card number over the phone, often having to yell it into the receiver two or more times to a staffer that could not hear me over the noise of the kitchen.

It also made me love a restaurant to which I had always been partial even more. Cava is a Mediterranean-style salad bowl and pita restaurant that is similar to Chipotle in terms of how you can select exactly what is in your meal. I've been going there for several years with my wife, Caroline. Before the pandemic, we had made a routine of going to the restaurant after work and dining in. But there was a problem: the restaurant was always freezing. Even in the middle of summer in Maryland, where it can get up to ninety degrees with 100 percent humidity, we were always freezing inside. It became an ongoing joke. We nicknamed it "Tundra," and we would often bring sweaters with us when we ate there year-round. We shivered through many dinners, but because we liked the food so much, we tolerated the subzero conditions.

During COVID-19, I explored Cava's online ordering site for the first time and just fell in love with it. It was so much easier to pay online, walk in the store, and pick it up. And bonus: we could eat in the warmth of our own home. What made it even better was that the app remembered your order, so you just hit repeat when you want to eat there again. I'm the type of guy who eats the same thing every time I go to a restaurant, so that option was magic to me. Caroline likes to shake it up a bit and order something slightly different each time, but the app made it very easy to modify past orders. Now when it's time for Cava, I just open up the website, repeat the order, and drive up to the restaurant and pick it up. Even when the dining room opens again, chances are we'll be placing our orders online. The convenience of online ordering apps is another dynamic to which the virus awakened us. Great food with easy ordering is an unbeatable combo.

## DEATH TO THE DRIVE-THROUGH LINE

Another app that's redefining dynamics? Chick-Fil-A. It's revolutionizing the future of the traditional drive-through line at fast-food restaurants. My Chick-Fil-A always had wildly long drive-through lines. It wasn't unusual for me to wait forty-five minutes to order and receive my food. Meanwhile, the Chick-Fil-A app makes it easy to order and stores your credit card and order history as well. You can then repeat an order or place a new one and just pull into a prenumbered spot in the parking lot where they will bring out your food when you arrive.

Why wait in a line of creeping cars and yell your order through a crackling speaker system? It's time to declare death to the fast-food drive-through line!

Systems like these also cut down on errors and waste for the proprietor, as the order can go directly into the kitchen without any confusion or losing anything in translation as the message is transferred from worker to worker. It is this kind of online ordering that the pandemic helped make mainstream and will likely become part of the new normal for years to come.

## THE PREVALENCE OF MEAL DELIVERY SERVICES

I believe the market for fresh delivery food will continue to expand as well, particularly as people are adapting to doing all their shopping and ordering from home. Caroline started getting Great Harvest shakes and veggie bowls shipped to our house during the pandemic. It is a fantastic company selling smoothies customized to you and delivered to your home. When you're ready, you simply throw them in a blender with a little bit of water, and you're good to go. With numerous options, you're not locked into having the same breakfast every morning either. You just order what you want online, and they ship it in a frozen container that arrives the next day.

Businesses that offer meal delivery services with a hassle-free order entry interface, quick shipments, fresh food, and little prep are going to do really well in the post-corona economy. Companies like Home Chef, Fresh and Easy, Hello Fresh, Sunbasket, and Dinnerly have the potential to thrive, especially as more people work from home and can easily receive shipments at any time of day now.

As the circumstances of our lives continue to change, savvy consumers are reinventing how they shop, cook, and consume food as well. With that in mind, it may be time to ask yourself why you've always done things the way you have and whether you might benefit from making and executing a new plan that takes advantage of developing dynamics.

As we continue our discussion of the long-term dynamics brought on by coronavirus, we must talk about a hot topic in business and beyond: events.

## Events

Since the virus began, many have said that events will never be the same again. Some have even gone as far as claiming that in-person events and programs are a thing of the past. I disagree. While events may take a while to come back up to where they were pre-pandemic due to the panic and fear that has ensued, they won't be gone forever. Put simply, people want to connect with one another, and in-person events are the best way to do that.

Corporate events will become even more prevalent as virtual professional relationships grow. They will become an important means of connection, especially for virtual-first organizations. As such, I believe companies will be more generous with their travel budgets, allowing employees to attend more events—something they may have been hesitant to do in the past. Employees will no longer have to work as hard to sell their managers on the idea of a business trip or retreat. While they may have needed three or four good reasons to travel in the past, simply explaining that they'd like to meet with another team member may be enough. Further, as I mentioned previously, without in-office perks and the benefits of socialization, companies will be looking for ways to keep employees happy and satisfied, and events are a great way to do that.

While events won't disappear, we may very well see the size and focus of many gatherings change—particularly in the corporate space. Prior to the virus, we were seeing large trade shows struggle with attendance. I think so much of this is due to the widespread amount of resources available online—there's not as much of a need to see products in person. That may mean reaching a smaller, more specialized audience with events that add more value in the form of education.

> Apply the iconoclast formula—ask why things are the way they are, make a plan to capitalize on the current dynamic, and then execute on that plan.

If you are in the events business, unlike retail, you don't have to fear the long-term impact of the virus. While 2020 and 2021 will still probably be tough years as people recover from so much panic and worry about a resurgence of the virus, things will turn around eventually.

And whether you're addressing a particular issue from the perspective of a CEO with a product or service to sell or as a consumer looking to improve your lifestyle, remember, there is always room to innovate. Apply the iconoclast formula—ask why things are the way they are, make a plan to capitalize on the current dynamic, and then execute on that plan. Chances are, you'll have a better solution for a different—and more promising—tomorrow.

# Part 7 Summary and Questions

## CHAPTER SUMMARY

- The coronavirus may well be the official end for many brick-and-mortar retail businesses as we know them.

- With new dynamics in place, online ordering and food delivery will be part of the new normal. Food providers that do not offer this service will lose to those who have made the process as easy and convenient as possible.

- Contrary to popular belief, in-person events won't be gone forever. Rather, they'll make a full comeback—though successful ones may require some different considerations.

## QUESTIONS TO CONSIDER

- What types of products do you still like to buy at traditional brick-and-mortar stores? What keeps you coming back to make your purchases in person?

- What would persuade you to shop elsewhere?

- Can you think of a company for which a change in the buying experience could lead to more success?

- Have you evaluated the purchasing and lifestyle decisions you make as a consumer? Are there any areas of your life that could benefit from the application of the iconoclast formula?

- How do you envision events in your industry or life happening in the future? Are you eager to get back? Nervous? Hungry for change? Are there any adjustments that would need to be made for you to feel comfortable returning?

## C O N C L U S I O N

Throughout this book, we've explored the impact of COVID-19, the novel coronavirus first seen in 2019. We discussed the way governments locally and globally reacted with panic, shutting down the economy and ushering in a wave of new dynamics that will continue to transform the way we live and work for years to come.

My belief is that novel viruses are essentially never going to go away—even after the primary threat of COVID-19 subsides. Instead, they will become part of normal consideration and planning. As I mentioned, I think human sickness will end up as a dimension of the current climate. Just like we have code-orange and red air-quality days and pollen and allergen alerts in addition to traditional rain, wind, sun, and temperature updates, we will take sickness into account as a potential environmental hazard too. We will monitor it and act accordingly, wearing a mask in public, social distancing, or engaging in more frequent handwashing and sanitizing when rates of infection go up. The cost of this pandemic has just been too significant and far-reaching to forget about it. A new normal is forming.

As we navigate a future that may seem bleak, though, we must recognize the opportunities in front of us—opportunities that iconoclasts are poised to see and take advantage of. One could argue that the pandemic has accelerated the adoption of new technology in almost every dimension of life, resulting in an ocean of new opportunities—especially for those who know how to capitalize on them.

With that in mind, we have discussed the definition of an iconoclast—someone who challenges the prescribed or established way of doing things, finds a better way, creates a plan for change, and executes it. We have highlighted the three primary traits of iconoclasts: they are creative thinkers, engineers of their own lives, and have the discipline and drive to make things better.

Like many skills, iconoclasm is a muscle. It becomes stronger with attention and practice. You can improve your ability to question everything around you and think creatively, engineer your future, and apply the kind of discipline necessary to succeed. That is, if you're passionate about doing so.

By now, you have a strong understanding of how these traits—and the iconoclast formula—position iconoclasts to succeed in their personal and professional lives, as well as in the challenging times presented by COVID-19 and any difficult circumstances that may lie ahead.

While the coronavirus panic established many new dynamics, some of which we've covered in this book, iconoclasm existed long before the start of the virus—and will persist far after it ends. And with this guide to adopting an iconoclast perspective and mode of operating, you'll be prepared to tackle whatever comes your way.